F*ck, I'm Bored!

Activity Book For Adults

Featuring 100 Fucking Adult Activities: Coloring, Sudoku, Dot-to-Dot, Word Searches, Mazes, Fallen Phrases, Math Logic, Word Tiles, Spot the Difference, Where the Fuck did the Other Half Go, Nanograms, Brick-by-Fucking-Brick, Word Scramble, and Much More!

Thank you for your purchase, assholes!!
I hope you enjoy this fucking book!!

Please consider leaving a review and checking out my
Amazon collection!

Contact me to get a free printable PDF of activities at:
http://www.tamaraladamsauthor.com/free-printable-activity-book-pdf/

tamaraadamsauthor@gmail.com

http://www.amazon.com/T.L.-Adams/e/B00YSROGC4

www.tamaraladamsauthor.com

https://twitter.com/@TamaraLAdams

https://www.facebook.com/TamaraLAdamsAuthor/

https://www.pinterest.com/tamara-l-adams-author/

Solve this bitch of a maze: Start in the center dot and get the fuck out!

Answer on page 101

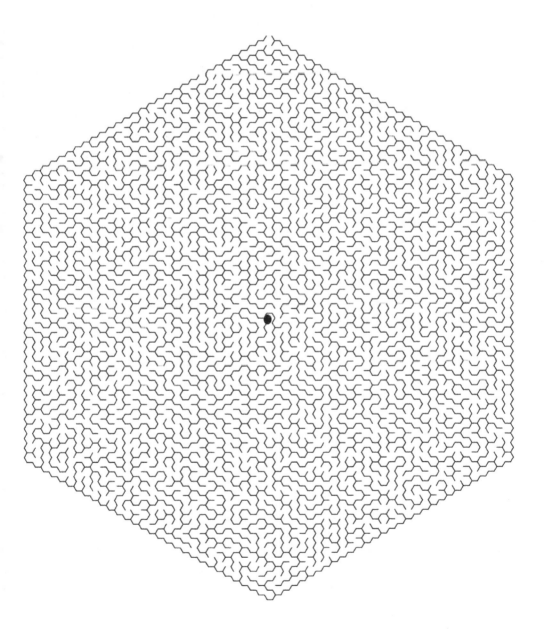

Think these pictures are the same? Think again, bitch! Circle the 10 differences.

Answer on page 101

2

Search for the goddamn words in the list

Arse	Bastard	Assnugget
Boob	Caveman	Cockmaster
Egoist	Fucker	Ignoramus
Flake	Monkey	Pervert
Jerk	Grouch	Whore
Snob	Sadist	Oger

Answer on page 101

```
W Y         B X O       H P Z       D Z B       L W D
D D U         S D Q       Y G L       S Z E       G O X
  G L F         B I L       H R F       L I E       T N G
    W I   L       W Y K       V O C       V X E       X B W
S       N K A       I E B       A U O       S O R       Q I
E N       Q M K       B K O       C C C       Z D O         V
B E O       C K E       A N O       Y H K       R J H
  N T B       A E E       I O B       F S M       E Z W
    U E W       V P S       O M H       G F A       G L G
I       R G S       E J R       Y T Z       S U S       O F
A T       P G C       M C A       Z R L       T C T       T
O C N       P U B       A F S       O E M       R K E
  K A E       Z N H       N D A       E V G       U E R
    R V L       U S F       C X D       D R W       N R A
G       E E I       J S X       U Q I       O E E       L E
A W       J Q C       R A Y       G Z S       I P T       R
M Q G       S H V       I P J       J H T       Z J L
  J K B       Q B O       G S Y       I K W       L G G
    I W A       P T Z       N U E       Z S H       X U S
L       C V S       Y P W       O I G       N C G       T B
C U       Z P T       U S I       R Y O       R G I       R
O Q H       X D A       F F Q       A B I       K B O
  V R G       M X R       L K R       M J S       Y R S
    T G L       N L D       O W S       U Q T       V O L
      J H A       M B E       M Q Y       S E Q       G X
```

3

Draw some fucking lines from 100 to 193 to see a sweet fucking picture! Ignore the extra shit.

Answer on page 101

Ever play Sudoku? I bet your sorry ass hasn't!
These are the goddamn rules.

Answer on page 101

Numbers from 1 to 9 are inserted into sets that have 9 x 9 = 81 squares in whole. Every number can be used just once in every 3x3 block, column and row, so don't reuse that shit.

- Every number can be used just once in the blocks of 3 x 3 = 9 square blocks. Use a number more than once, you fuck everything up.
- Each row of 9 numbers ought to contain all digits 1 through 9 in any order, so don't fucking miss any.
- Every column of 9 numbers should comprise all digits 1 through 9 in any order. Hope you can fucking count.

Here's a hint for your stupid ass: One way to figure out which numbers can go in each space is to use "process of elimination" by checking to see which other numbers are already included within each square – remember, no duplicates, asshole.

8	2						9	
9		6		3	2		5	
	4			1				6
8	3							
2		9				8		4
						5	2	
4				6			1	
	9		8	5		3		7
	7						8	2

This picture's fucked to hell! Draw each image to its corresponding square to fix that shit.

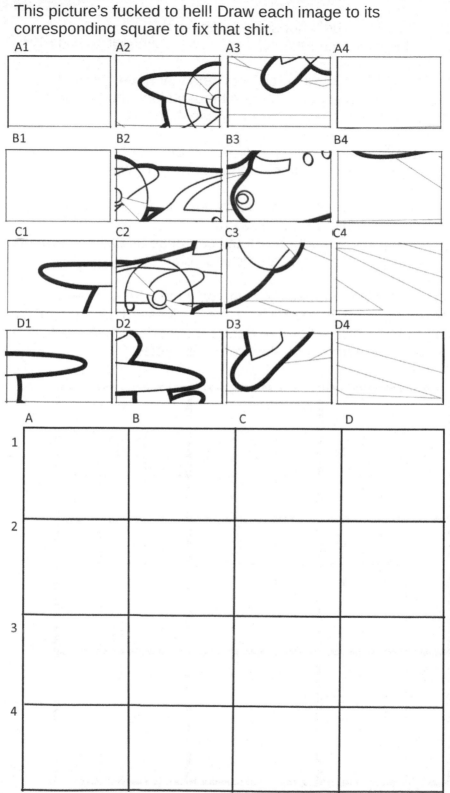

Answer on page 101

None of these words make any fucking sense. Unscramble each of the words.
Take the letters that appear in numbered boxes and unscramble them to reveal a word that describes anyone who hasn't bought this book.

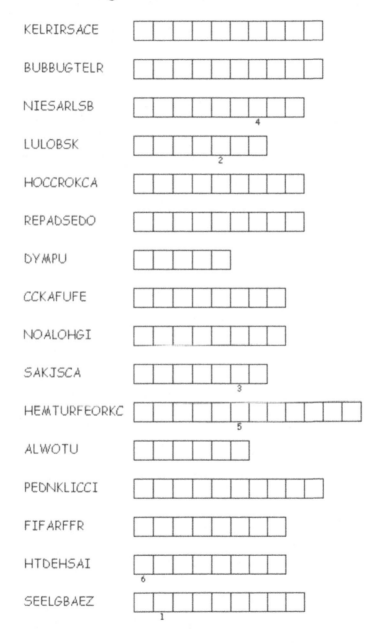

KELRIRSACE

BUBBUGTELR

NIESARLSB

LULOBSK

HOCCROKCA

REPADSEDO

DYMPU

CCKAFUFE

NOALOHGI

SAKJSCA

HEMTURFEORKC

ALWOTU

PEDNKLICCI

FIFARFFR

HTDEHSAI

SEELGBAEZ

Answer on page 102

Draw some fucking lines from 100 to 149 to reveal a sweet fucking word! Ignore the extra shit.

Answer on page 102

258   162   201   278   240   276
218   147
146   243
152   157   233   248   264   245   244
238   246   223   233   246   249   242   238   160
254   243 245   247   250   237   272   237
148   253   149
251   257   254   255   274   239
265   279   255
270   143   142   236
271   226   254   275   166   229
230   248   185   249
262   161   264   168   167   165
258   151   209   236
256   238   145   144   250   259   265
241   257   169   272   163
242   269   239   212   243
140   241   247   141   269   266
259   239   214   210
244   139   208   171   138   241   267
253   170
239   222   239   260
159   236   195   268   164
237   237   226   261   172   250 133 245
132   259   277   256   263
236   196   271   156
268   225   197   134
235   131   211   239   130   135   236   174   263
212   275   240
217   210   198   188   175
235   266   153   173   238
207 209   236   248 176   177
279   278   261
279   215   213   271   189 199   187   178
214   186   181   179
234   128   238   129   136   273   260   137   180
265   276   184   183   182
228   200   126   213
260   127   154   217   264   206   215   269   275   194
263   278   256   218   273   267   237   249
277   116   216   231   124   193
270   220   261   247   123   266   274   246   252
115   117   270   108   107   125   274   252
262   237   228   224   100
150   114   118   238   122   225   190   192
224   252   244   242   106   202   251
234   119   227   191
272   113   257   216   109   255   205   101   231   211   158
120   121   258   105   220   268
267   204   110   104   273   102   229
112   111   227   203   240   222
230   251   276   103
155   253

8

Answer on page 102

How many fucking  make up the goddamn giant fist? (Don't count the one up your ass)

Solve this tit of a maze: Start in the nipple and work your way the fuck out!

Answer on page 102

Letter Tiles

Answer on page 102

I can't understand what the fuck any
of this shit says.
Move the motherfucking tiles around to
make the correct phrase.
The three letters on each tile must
stay together and in the given order,
so don't try to cheat, asshole!

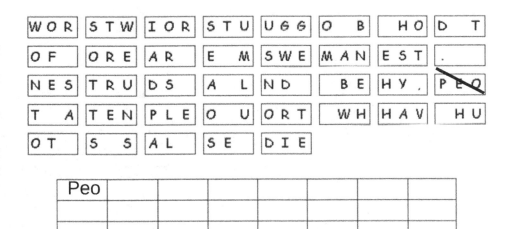

Peo							

One fucking asshole always has to stand out in a crowd. Find the cunt that's different from the rest.

Answer on page 102

A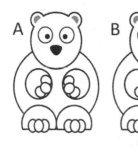
B
C
D
E

F
G
H
I
J

K
L
M
N
O

P
Q
R
S
T

U
V
W
X
Y

The fucked rules of a cryptogram puzzle:

You are given a shit piece of text where each letter is substituted with a irrelevant damn number and you need to fucking decide which letter in the native alphabet is being coded by the numbers you are given.

You need to use logic and knowledge of the letters and words of our goddamn language to crack this shit.

Answer on page 102

A hint for you lazy fuckers:
One of the words is *mean*

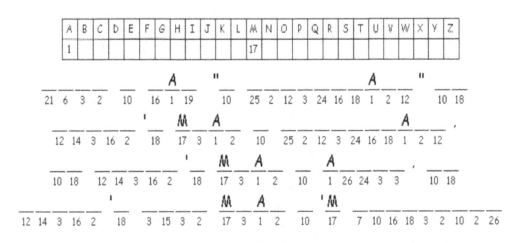

The goal of this puzzle is to figure out how the fuck you fit the numbered hexagons into the motherfucking rectangle of hexagons (that's a fuckload of geometry right there!) without changing their goddamnshape or breaking them into fucking smaller pieces.

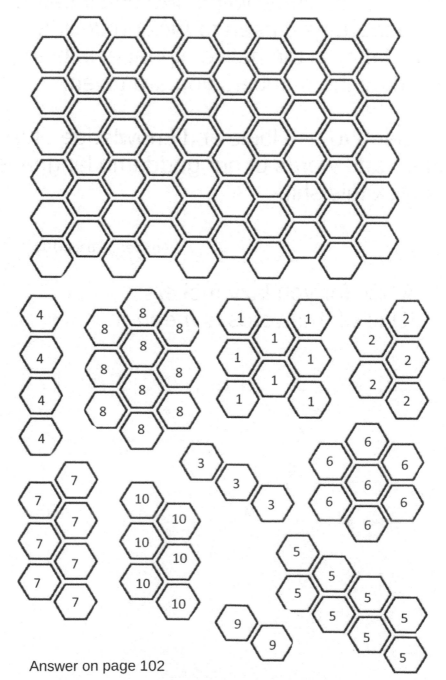

Answer on page 102

I can't read these fucking words. Unscramble the fuck out of them. Take the letters that appear in numbered boxes to reveal the word that describes your ex.

SRMTAASES

TICBH

RABTINRAF

CANNIBLA

CKCEHNI

DORDAHLET

ODBUM

COGFUNNIKG

PUYML

DAETNLAERHN

COILIDK

PIPRER

TESRIAHET

SEIDNRLW

J | | | | |
1 2 3 4 5

Answer on page 103

Color your ass off!

Ever play Sudoku? I bet your ridiculous ass hasn't!
Here are the mother fucking rules.   Answer on page 103

Numbers from 1 to 9 are inserted into sets that have 9 x 9 = 81 squares in whole. Every number can be used just once in every 3x3 block, column and row, so don't reuse that shit.

- Every number can be used just once in the blocks of 3 x 3 = 9 square blocks. Use a number more than once, you fuck shit up.
- Each row of 9 numbers ought to contain all digits 1 through 9 in any order, so don't leave out any numbers, asshole.
- Every column of 9 numbers should comprise all digits 1 through 9 in any order. Hope you got all that that shit.

Here's a hint jackass: One way to figure out which numbers can go in each space is to use "process of elimination" by checking to see which other numbers are already included within each square – remember, no duplicates, dumbass.

	8	7	6				3	
5			1		8	7		2
		3		2				
	1					6		
	9	5				3	1	
		6					4	
				7		1		
6		8	5		3			7
	3				4	5	8	

The damn goal consists of finding the black boxes in each grid.

The numbers given on the side and top of the grid indicate the numbers of consecutive black boxes in each line or column. Got that, bitches?

Here's a goddamn example: 3,3 on the left of a line indicates that there is, from left to right, a block of 3 black boxes then a block of 3 black boxes on this line. Have I lost your ass yet?

To solve the puzzle, you need to determine which cells will be black and which will be fucking empty. Determining which cells are to be left empty (called spaces) is as important as determining which to fill (called boxes). Later in the solving process, the spaces help determine where a clue (continuing block of boxes and a number in the legend) may spread. Solvers usually use a dot or a cross to mark cells they are certain are spaces.

It is also important never to fucking guess. Only cells that can be determined by damn logic should be filled. An example is shown here:

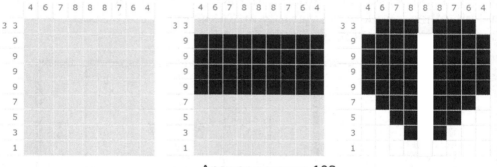

Answer on page 103

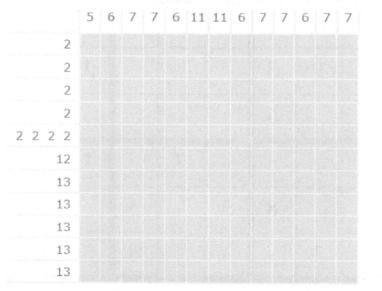

Number Blocks

Answer on page 103

Try to fill in the missing numbers if you can, bitch!

The missing numbers are integers (that means it's a whole number, dumbass) between 0 and 9.
The numbers in each row add up to the totals to the right. The numbers in each column add up to the totals along the bottom. Numbers can be repeated, so don't get fucking confused! Keep it simple, stupid.
The diagonal lines also add up the totals to the right.
Good fucking luck!

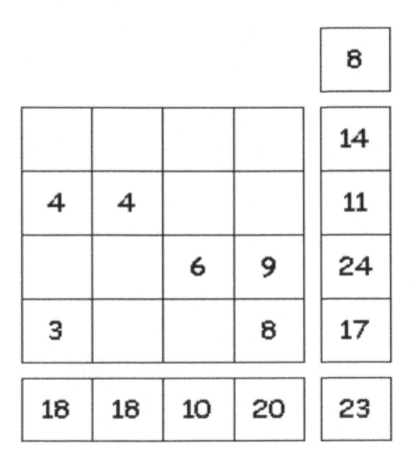

Holy shit, that's a lot of circles! Someone should keep track of this shit. Count up all the circles in the egg. Answer on page 103

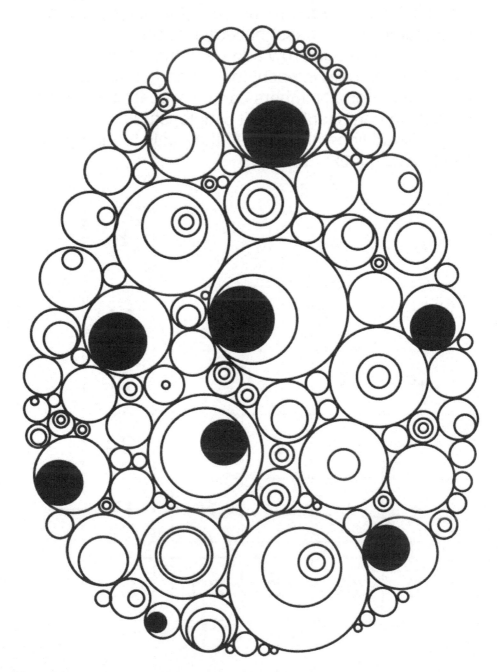

Draw some motherfucking lines from 100 to 156 to reveal a magnificent fucking picture!
Ignore the extra shit.

Answer on page 103

287
248   259   247   293   238   297   296   265
273   295
267   270   192   265   279   263   254   264
268   111   112   253   214   261   266   168   235
                                266   217
249   246   273   113   261   215   251   191
                172 268   114   115
210   110   174   271   275   258   204   181   243   257
109   169   274 275 171   223   190   282   250   263
205   175   229   228   272   195   189 182
230   227
108   176   270 194   196   188   183   283   116
243   232   202   187
245   151   233   252
249   152   303   201   197   186 185   184   247   117
222   107   153   254 251   300   276   180
106   290   200   198   170 122
248   239   255   150   241   199   285 193   177   118
170   240   239   237 134   246   277   178   221   123   218
240   154   212   149   279   302   164 220   219   280
105   133   129   252   119
225   155 100 101   160   239   143   242   135   121
238   104   156   291   159   244   136   231   244   226   124
103   102   245   142   236   132   253   157   120
224   148   144   238   161
236   141   137   131   262   130   128   125
259   241   147
286   166 260   146   145   140   167   138   213   127   237   236
165   237   126
278   208   242 207   256   269   139   274   211   163 158   255   267
173   206   236   239   277   162
264   301   294   276   238   272   260   269   234
258   250   289   288   257   281
262   271   292   237   299   298   284   256

Fallen Phrases

Answer on page 103

A fallen phrase is a fucked puzzle where all the letters have fallen to the bottom. They got jacked up on their way down, but remain in the same row. Complete this horse shit by filling the letters in the column they fall under. You start by filling in the one-letter columns, because those clearly don't have anywhere else to go in their column, dumbass.
Don't make this shit harder than it has to be.
Also try filling in common one-, two- and three-letter words. I even gave your lucky ass an example.

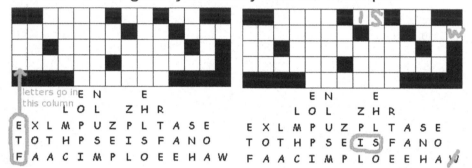

letters go in this column

```
      E  N        E                    E  N        E
      L  O  L     Z  H  R              L  O  L     Z  H  R
E  X  L  M  P  U  Z  P  L  T  A  S  E  E  X  L  M  P  U  Z  P  L  T  A  S  E
T  O  T  H  P  S  E  I  S  F  A  N  O  T  O  T  H  P  S  E  I  S  F  A  N  O
F  A  A  C  I  M  P  L  O  E  E  H  A  W  F  A  A  C  I  M  P  L  O  E  E  H  A  W
```

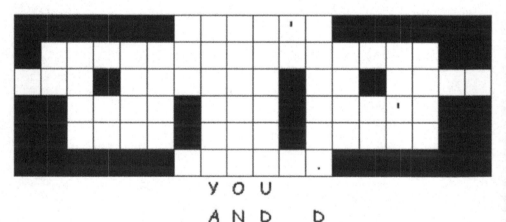

```
               Y  O  U
               A  N  D     D
      E     A  A  W  O  R  E     T  E           R
      K  S  H  P  L  O  I  N     M  O  E  T  T
      R  I  N  E  N  P  D  F  Y  T  S  W  N  A  S
A  D  W  H  O  W  R  I  E  R  S  S  O  N  T  A  K  E
```

Where'd the other motherfucking half go?
Draw that shit.

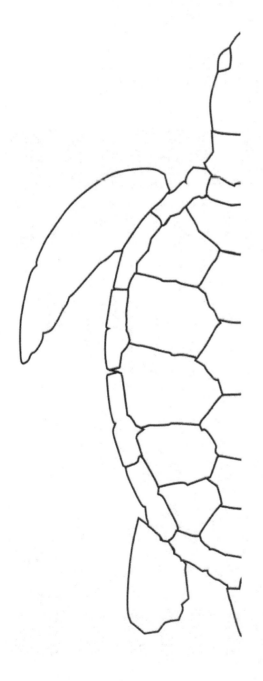

How many Dammits can you find, god
dammit?

Answer on page 103

Solve the wanker of a maze. Start at the opening on the left side and work your way to the center of that shit.

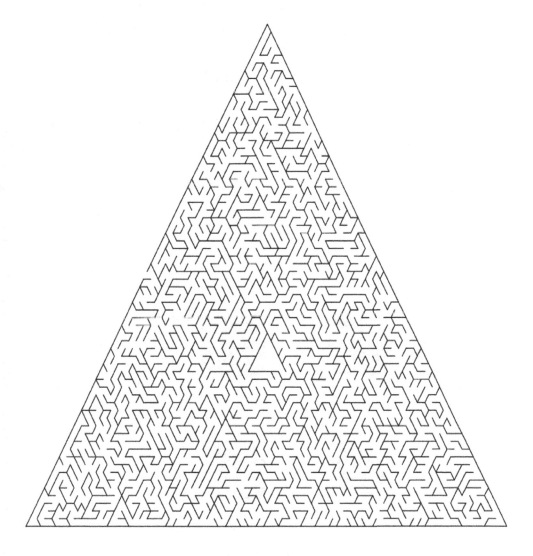

Answer on page 103

Math Squares

Answer on page 103

Try to fill in the missing numbers, bitch!

Use the numbers 1 through 9 to complete the equations. Not good at math? You're fucked.

Each number is only used once, got it?

Each row is a math equation. Good luck with that shit. Work from left to right.

That's not all! Each column is a math equation, too. Surprise, bitch! Work from top to bottom.

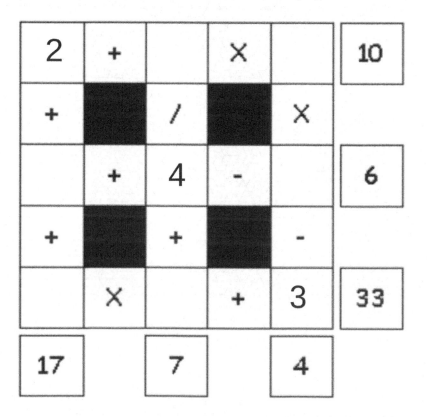

Color that shit up!

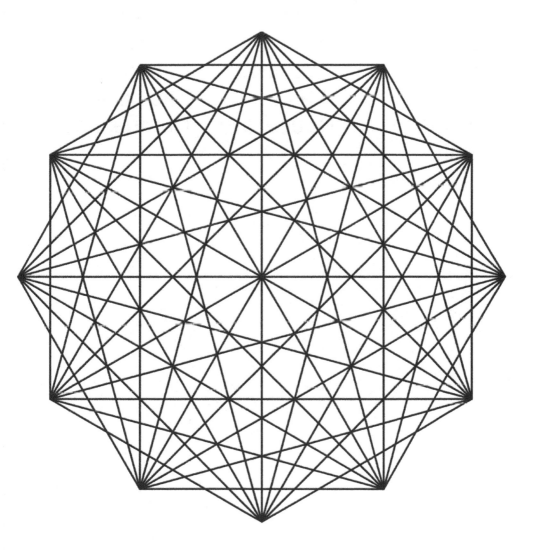

Search for all these shitty words in the Triangle below.

Answer on page 104

Crap   Poop   Defecation
Dung   Manure   Discharge
Feces   Excretion Excrement
Stool   Waste   Feculence
Shart   Deuce   NumberTwo
Shit

```
                              J  N
                              V  N
                           G  A  F  X
                           W  X  F  D
                        A  S  P  E  Z  K
                        u  H  O  C  C  K
                     H  S  A  O  E  N  K  A
                     L  J  R  P  S  M  N  O
                  Y  P  Y  T  S  O  S  N  C  D
                  Y  G  B  E  T  L  O  M  G  O
               M  E  X  X  X  L  A  O  E  L  V  C
               L  E  Z  K  N  L  E  R  O  H  R  V
            Q  J  T  R  U  U  B  X  A  T  T  C  E  H
            F  E  S  K  K  M  S  C  M  B  D  S  M  I
         D  C  V  A  C  Y  B  O  R  N  J  E  F  Z  C  T
         X  M  K  W  G  M  E  G  E  Z  S  S  L  L  X  D
      u  L  Y  F  C  P  G  R  J  T  B  X  H  O  Q  Q  A  F
      I  R  T  C  O  L  V  T  B  I  R  P  Q  L  V  F  X  H
   K  F  u  W  I  W  C  A  W  G  O  E  C  U  E  D  M  P  E  F
   N  Q  Y  X  T  H  Y  E  O  R  N  S  O  N  J  G  A  M  Z  B
H  P  F  K  E  G  S  S  L  Q  W  X  X  F  O  S  R  R  R  P  R  L
H  L  Q  X  Y  D  Z  I  R  G  D  M  E  J  I  C  Z  S  A  P  V  C
K  Z  S  C  H  J  K  P  I  U  I  M  J  X  G  T  J  I  Y  B  H  B  L  T
H  S  R  G  N  U  D  E  Q  O  Y  I  R  F  S  A  R  A  Y  F  G  C  M  V
K  X  E  C  Y  J  S  X  L  K  T  T  L  N  F  B  C  J  M  E  G  Z  E  S  P  X
X  M  E  P  R  J  I  L  V  X  Y  K  F  Q  Z  X  E  H  Z  R  C  U  J  M  I  O
J  E  G  Q  K  A  B  V  Y  S  R  E  R  U  N  A  M  F  I  O  S  E  A  Q  R  E  D  G
N  M  Q  F  V  u  S  K  U  O  M  D  F  E  C  U  L  E  N  C  E  L  F  Z  N  A  Q  O
T  A  Y  T  H  S  W  J  P  G  E  J  U  X  R  X  L  E  D  D  E  O  K  V  K  E  Z  N  Y  I
J  F  G  V  B  S  Q  K  C  N  I  S  T  G  X  X  P  Q  A  F  Z  R  Y  E  R  M  G  V  A  M
```

Letter Tiles

Answer on page 104

I can't understand this shit!

Move the fucking tiles around to make the correct phrase.

The three letters on each tile must stay together and in the given order, so don't try to cheat, motherfucker!

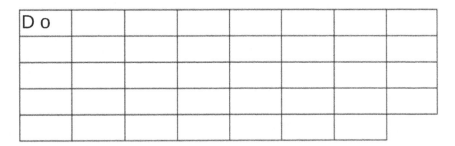

One fucking cunt always has to be the difficult one. Find the asshole that's different from the rest.

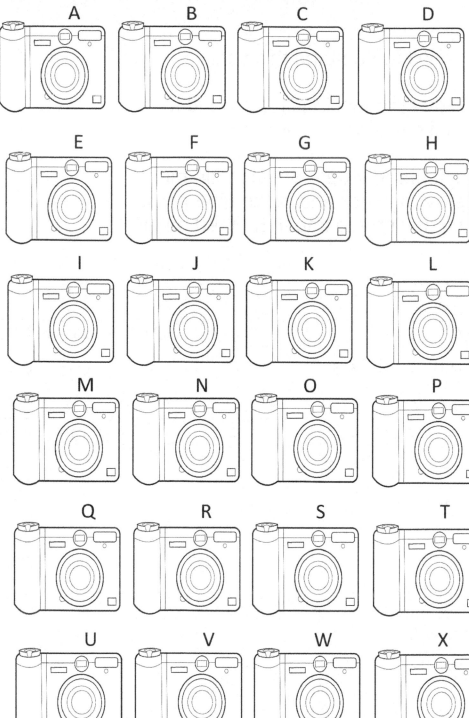

Answer on page 104

Fallen Phrases

Answer on page 104

A fallen phrase is a fucked puzzle where all the letters have fallen to the bottom. They got jacked up on their way down, but remain in the same row. Complete this horse shit by filling the letters in the column they fall under. You start by filling in the one-letter columns, because those clearly don't have anywhere else to go in their column, dumbass. Don't make this shit harder than it has to be. Also try filling in common one-, two- and three-letter words. I even gave your lucky ass an example.

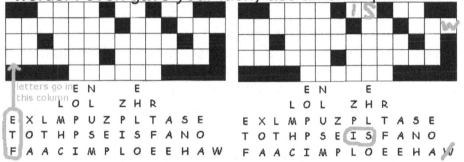

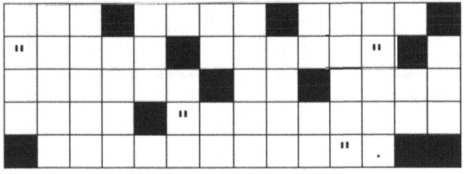

Ever play Sudoku? I bet your sorry ass hasn't!
These are the goddamn rules.

Answer on page 104

Numbers from 1 to 9 are inserted into sets that have 9 x 9 = 81 squares in whole. Every number can be used just once in every, 3x3 block, column and row, so don't reuse that shit.

- Every number can be used just once in the blocks of 3 x 3 = 9 square blocks. Use a number more than once, you fuck everything up.
- Each row of 9 numbers ought to contain all digits 1 through 9 in any order, so don't fucking miss any.
- Every column of 9 numbers should comprise all digits 1 through 9 in any order. Hope you can fucking count.

Here's a hint for your stupid ass: One way to figure out which numbers can go in each space is to use "process of elimination" by checking to see which other numbers are already included within each square – remember, no duplicates, asshole.

		8						
	7	1					2	
4			6		9		5	
2	3	7	8		4			5
	8						7	
1			2		3	9	8	4
	4		9		2			7
	5					3	4	
						6		

Solve the maze, bitch. Start in the slit at the top
and get the fuck down to the bottom.

How many fucking cheery-ass butterflies can you find?

Answer on page 104

I can't read any of these damn words. Unscramble this shit. Then use the letters that appear in the numbered boxes to reveal words that describes this fucking book.

Answer on page 105

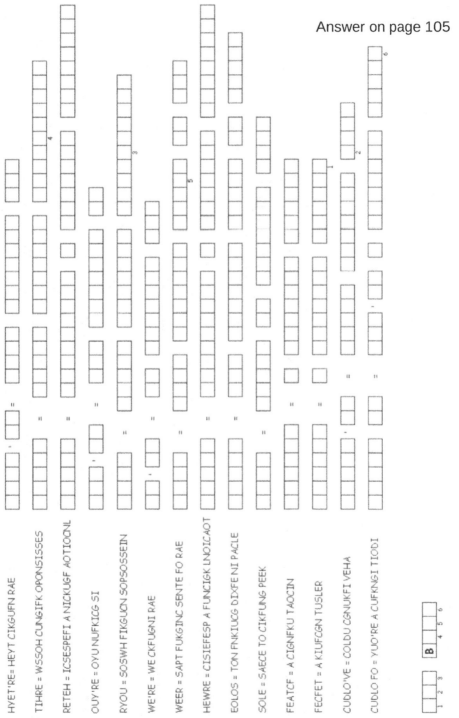

HYET'RE = HEYT CIKGUFN RAE

TIHRE = WSSOH CUNGIFK OPONSISSES

RETEH = ICSESPEFI A NICKUGF AOTIOCNL

OUY'RE = OYU NUFKIIG SI

RYOU = SOSWH FIKGUCN SOPSOSSEIN

WE'RE = WE CKFUGNI RAE

WEER = SAPT FUKGINC SENTE FO RAE

HEWRE = CISIEFESP A FUNCIGK LNOICAOT

EOLOS = TON FNKIUCG DIXFE NI PACLE

SOLE = SAECE TO CIKFUNG PEEK

FEATCF = A CIGNFKU TAOCIN

FECFET = A KIUFCGN TUSLER

CUDLO'VE = COLDU CGNUKFI VEHA

CUDLO FO = YUO'RE A CUFKNGI TIODI

One fucking asshole always has to be different. Find that cunt.

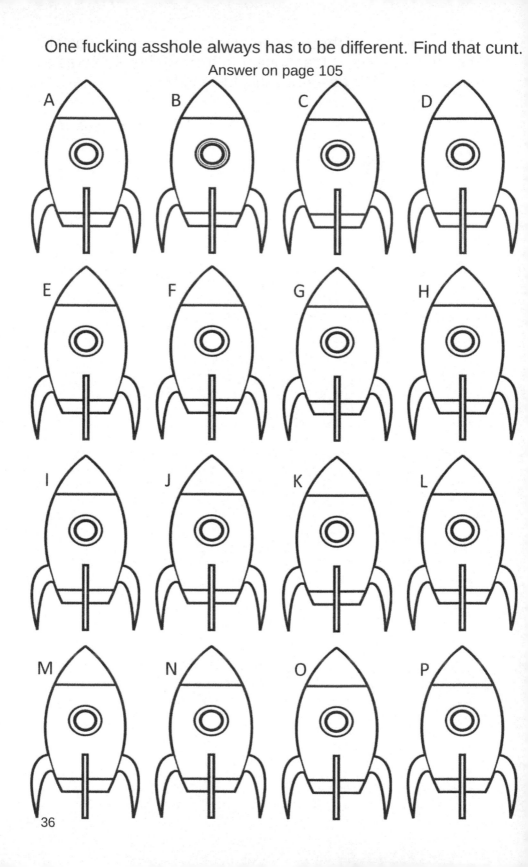

Answer on page 105

Search for the fucked up words, wanker.

Bandit   Boozer   Asskisser
Dummy   Cheater   Hillbilly
Eunuch   Sleaze   Monster
Fibber   Oldfart   Reject
Conman Varmint Weirdo

```
M Q X J P      S X T            A Y C    D U B K R
U H D O A      M X D            S L G    T Q T S E
M I H M Y      I D J            S L L    Z Q T A Z
V F C          D V G            K I F    U C O
U D U          R W E            I B K    Z L O
D T N          Z L B            S L C    J B B
A U U          Y W P            S L A    B T D
H I E          J Y A            E I E    U P I
P U L          V B M            R H P    O L C
A M M          I V E F B G E K Q E       Q N H
V C Q          R Q K V A R M I N T       S K V
S R B          W L M S R Z J W O Q       B G C
L D C          C R D            V L T    G J H
E P M          M E W            F D W    P M E
A U C          O J E            Y F N    H K A
Z N C          N E I            M A D    B B T
E K O          S C R            Z R U    V A E
C L R          T T D            Y T M    C N R
C C E          E D O            C F M    K D Y
O Q B          R F U            Q I Y    I I F
N I B          Q I Y            T H S    H T T
M T I X A                                D X B V Y
A R F V A                                O L G X B
N W J A A                                P L Y H C
```

The other half is gone, bitch.
You need to draw it back in or we are
all fucked!

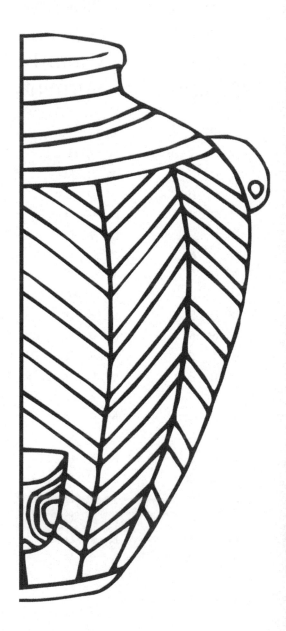

Connect the damn numbers from 100 to 139
The other fucking numbers are extra, so don't get fucked by them!

Answer on page 105

255   121   266
248   174   237   120   122   241
250   241   245   239
242   114   247   267
270   238   243   115   239   119   256   123
210   116   250   259
258   257   239   257   155   246
265   117   242   124
271 113   112   111   238   249   245
262   164   125   160   173   156
279   276   244   194
237   278   235   274   272   271   157
263   268   126   127   270   158
223   273   128
140   261   193
260   110   234   233   133   276   177
225   238   165   163   129
222   161   172   279   244
269   228   230   272 132   166
255   267   224   226   175   134   131   263   261
109   159   217   229   170   169   168 167   162   130
264   218   274
216   176   181   260   269
153   215   180   183   182   154
220   227   273
145   249   135   236   247   195
108   248   246   214   184
243   210   212   179   275   237
107   209   211   136   213   178   185   238   236
240   104   277
106   137   236   192
105   239   237   103   186   264   191
278   277
265   254   275   138   190   196
188   208   102   266   187
262   253   252   204   149   197
108   253   101   139   250 148   189   198
236   201   254   144   150
253   100   147   203   199   256
268   251   259   146   143
252   141   151
142   200
251   152   202

Think these pictures are the same? Think again, asshole!
Circle the 13 differences, then check to see if you're right.

Answer on page 105

Start in the middle and find your way the fuck out of this shit!

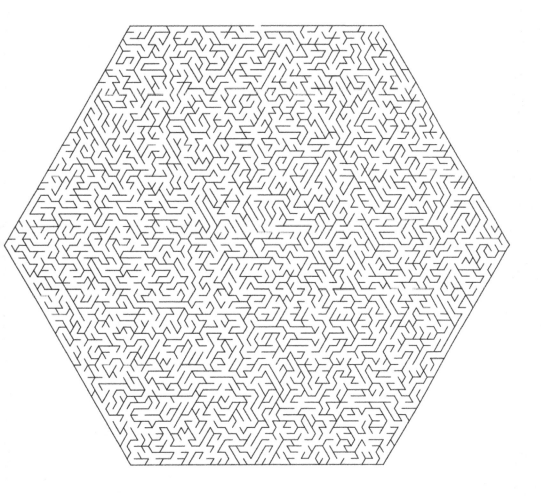

Connect the fucking numbers from 100 to 134

Answer on page 106

Don't let the extra damn numbers fool your dumb ass!

230
218 101 102   268   278   240   276   162
159   258   233 233 248 264   245   244   243
    138   242
238   246   223   137   246   238
257   254   243 245 247 249   237   237
    100 104 103   136   253   250
251   254   255 255   274   272   153
    265   279   239
                226   254 151   275   236
271   230   141
    270   105   106   248   185   166
262   111   249
        238   264   107 258   135   236   265   156
256   250   259   168 167
            241   212   257 169   272   139
    242   269   239   243
259   241   108   214   247   210   269   266
244   239   110 109   262   171   170   241   267
    239   253   222   195 239   260
158   237   226 261   268
    237   236 259   113 112   172   250   245
236   268   225   116   256   263   270
235   211 239   196   271   174
        157   212   210   197 275   236   263
    217   209 198 173   238 188 175   240
235   266   207   236 248 176   177
    279   215   114 115 278   261
209   271   189 199   187 178
150   238   214 213   260 186 181   179
    234   276 124 273   184 183 182 180
        228   265   123   125 200
260   161   217 264 206 117 269   275 194   213
263   122   215
    278   256   218   273   267   237 249 154
    277   216 121 231   118   201   193
270   220   261   266   274 246 252
    262   279   227   247 120   119 208   274   252
152   142   238   237 228   225 190   202 192
    234   224 252   244   242   191   251
272   140   155   216   126 227 127   211   146
        257   134   255 205   231
163   267   204   258 133 132 129 128   220
    144   251   160   229   229   148
        147 145 143 276   253   273   222
    165   164 131 130 240   203   149
42

This picture's fucking fucked! Draw each image to it's correct square to fix the the motherfucker.

Answer on page 106

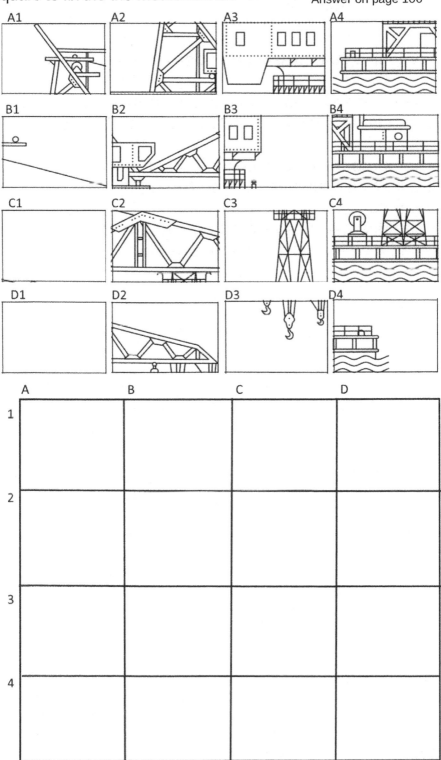

Number Blocks

Answer on page 106

Try to fill in the missing numbers if you can, bitch!

The missing numbers are between fucking 0 and 12.
The numbers in each row add up to the totals to the
right.
The numbers in each column add up to the totals along
the bottom. Numbers can be repeated, so do what you
gotta do!
The diagonal lines also add up the totals to the right.
Good fucking luck! You're gonna need it.

					47
14	12	9		10	53
			10		34
1		8		10	33
		1	3	1	19
9	13	1		0	24
31	41	31	34	26	29

Think these pictures are the same? You're wrong, bitch!
Circle the 10 differences.

Answer on page 106

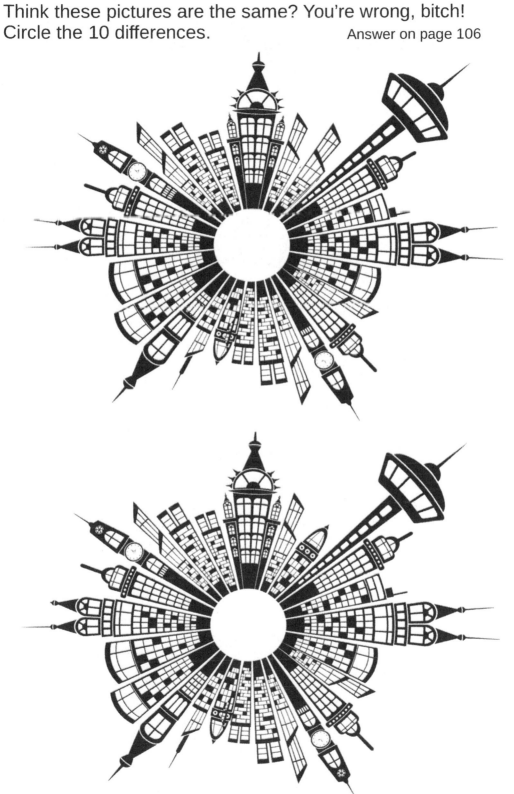

Have fun coloring, assholes!

Letter Tiles

Answer on page 107

This shit is fucked!

Move the jacked tiles around to
make the correct fucking phrase.

The three letters on each tile must
stay the fuck together and in the given order,
so don't try to cheat, you wanker!

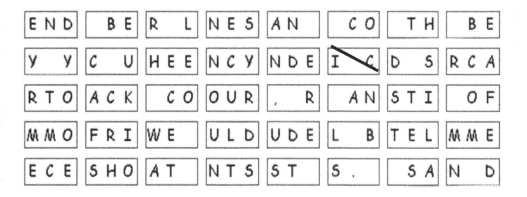

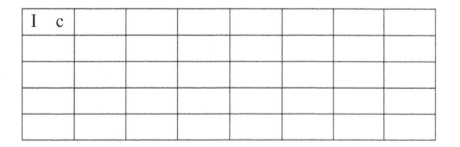

Search for the words, jackass

Baby	Clown	Asshole
Bum	Cretin	Grumpy
Fuck	Devil	Mutant
Nuts	Lucky	Pavian
Swine	Sod	Weezebag

```
                              F Q V
                        N W R O U U I C C
                    O K W B N X W G C T X X D
                  W Q G Y G B C D A M X W D A M A E
                T W M P J L I V E D S A Y A J Y Y O W
              C M U F D N E U W K T Y D S O C Q S V C L
              L M P V M A C J S M X B I A S X Y W V T H
            N O B A W H W Y I T U J Q P C F H I O M Y Y X
            U W R E U N J J C A W H K K O W A O E Q Y P I
          B P N X M H S Y P O X D P Q Z A B V E L E M F Z V
          F X K S N S Y O P W T J A M W Z C G E Y E T X T S
          S G D F O R T S A M K U A F Z Q A R Z M F V G C J
      U B L L Y Z D W V V H H C C W V K W U Z E H B L M O O
      R O E A U B H M O I N P K U J N R K M D A N Y O W C J
    M F M K Y H U A E A I B S L F D E G P I Y T I H M E C
      R O U U K S F Q N T U S G U Y X H Y Y Y A L W Z B
      S N R B F K O W E E Z E B A G T B Y G B Y A U S M
      A D D N M A P S N R Y U H I Y J F R H R Z Z J I Z
        N W L Q Y U M J C A S H Z W E N V C J B H U M
        V E Q X X K S E H M Z Z A S B Y A M U T A N T
          Q N T D P C F P P F A M H E B A B Y A R C
          T Z Y V Z T U V Q M T C Z T B K N M O V T
            K X M D S Y L M I J U A T Q L E O M S
              U F G P T Z Y L L F B E J T H V F
              R J N U J T T S G V N J B
                C E N Y L K W W A
                    Y P T
```

Answer on page 107

Find the motherfucker that's different from the rest.

Answer on page 107

A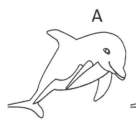
B
C
D

E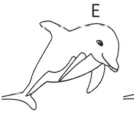
F
G
H

I
J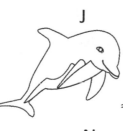
K
L

M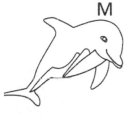
N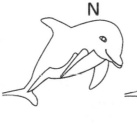
O
P

Q
R
S
T

U
V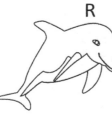
W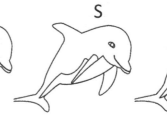
X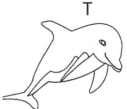

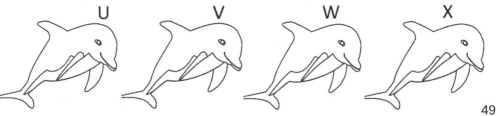

Fallen Phrases

Answer on page 107

A fallen phrase is a fucked puzzle where all the letters have fallen to the bottom. They got jacked up on their way down, but remain in the same row. Complete this fucked puzzle by filling the letters in the column they fall under. You start by filling in the one-letter columns, because those clearly don't have anywhere else to go in their column, jackbass. Don't make this shit harder than it has to be.

Also try filling in common one-, two- and three-letter words. I even gave your lucky ass an example.

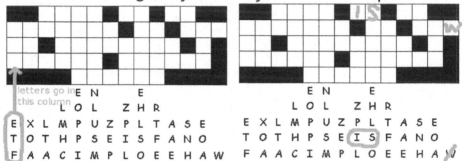

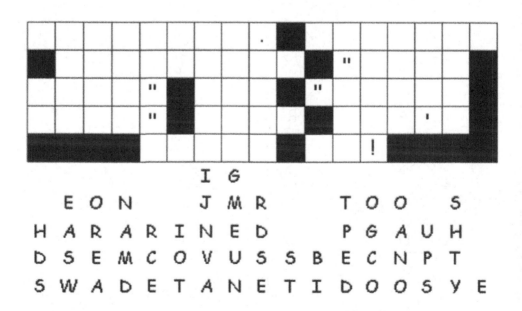

Math Squares

Answer on page 107

Try to fill in the missing numbers, wanker!

Use the numbers 1 through 16 to complete the equations. Not good at math…get your ass back to school.

Each number is only used once, so don't fuck it up!

Each row is a math equation, good luck with that shit. Work from left to right.

That's not all! Each column is also a math equation, too. Surprise, bitch. This is too much fucking math, but if your gonna do it, work from top to bottom.

		7		2			-14
−		+		×		×	
15	+		+		×	12	73
×		−		−		/	
	−	11	×		/		-25
+		+		−		−	
	−		−	5	−		-16
135		19		-6		10	

Answer on page 107

Solve the maze, asswipe. Start in the opening at the top and work your way to the opening at the goddamn bottom.

Ever play Sudoku? I bet you fucking haven't! These are the wanked rules.

Answer on page 107

Numbers from 1 to 9 are inserted into sets that have 9 x 9 = 81 squares in whole. Every number can be used just once in every, 3x3 block, column and row, so don't reuse the goddamn shit.

- Every number can be used just once in the blocks of 3 x 3 = 9 square blocks. Use a number more than once, your fucked.
- Each row of 9 numbers must fucking contain all digits 1 through 9 in any order, so don't fucking miss that shit.
- Every column of 9 numbers should comprise all digits 1 through 9 in any order. Hope you can fucking count, bitch.

Here's a hint for your stupid ass: One way to figure out which numbers can go in each space is to use "process of elimination" by checking to see which other numbers are already included within each square – remember, no duplicates, asshole.

				7	4	2		6
	2	4	6		3		7	
				2		5		9
						8		
	5		2		6		1	
		3						
2		5		1				
	1		4		5	9	6	
8		9	7	6				

Letter Tiles

Answer on page 107

What the fuck is this shit?!

Move the piece of shit tiles around to make the correct phrase.

The three letters on each tile must stay together and in the given order, so don't try to cheat, motherfucker!

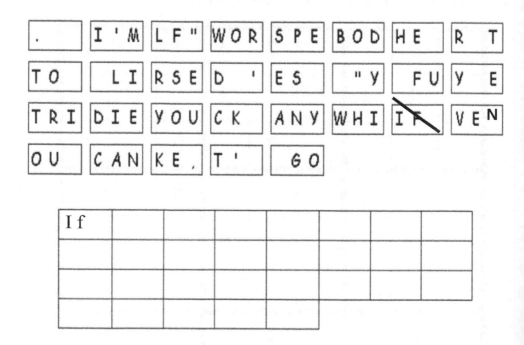

Think these pictures are the same? Wrong answer, asshole! Circle the 10 differences.

Answer on page 108

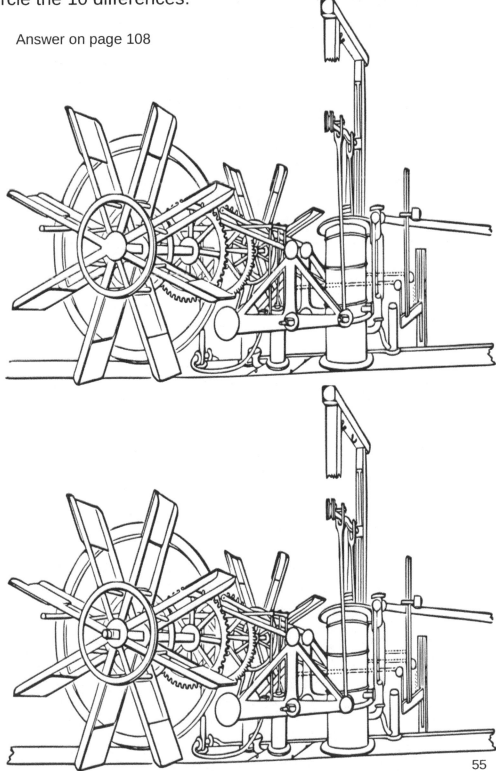

Draw some damn lines from 100 to 155
Don't let the extra numbers fuck you up!

Answer on page 108

254   255
274   275   169   273   271   211   270
236   253   252   250   247   213   210   114   207
230   272   251   156   266   241   239   115
244   242   253   215   215
212   249   246   112   209   248   116
235   234   237   248   254   265   255
247   243   245   243   277   213   210   251
239   168   252   249   211
224   231   236   241   262   251   250   238
244   242   264   157   158
238   240   239   237   111   260   162
226   235   237   249   246   163   117
214   238   110   268   217   248   225   164   264
228   236   239   246   245   243   262   259
220   109   236   257   266   265   166
191   108   227   258   231
227   237   241   165   236   268   118
223   228   240   277   240   239   237   167
229   264   234   274   226   275   272   256   171
107   239   229   173   172
222   149   272   274   174   275
217   273   142   271   175   119
245   218   262   159   271   237   120   176   273
150   134   270   238   124   177   192
242   214   106   279   276   133   126   125   193
224   190   225   160   135   278   279   206   194   178   253
277   212   263   127   276   121   179
238   279   151   143   161   278   203
105   191   238   122   270
263   278   148   141   136   261   132   263   123
276   265   260   269   267   128   204   180   181
102 103 104 152   216   199   131   261
153   147   193   140   130   129   269   267   195   250   244
101   260   269   267   233   268   137   259   202   196   182
154   144   138   258   201   197   220   183   255
155   259   146   145   216   223   200   198   185   184   170
100   252   195   257   189   186   233   254
222   261   257   188   187
218   256   247   256   205   190
192   230

Look! Another tit maze! Start in the center and work your way out at the top. Don't get fucking lost or your fucked.

Answer on page 108

How many fucking fucked up hearts can you find in the image?

Answer on page 108

Draw the other fucking half.

I can't read these piece of shit words. Unscramble the motherfuckers. Then use the damn letters that appear in numbered boxes to reveal a word that describes your boss.

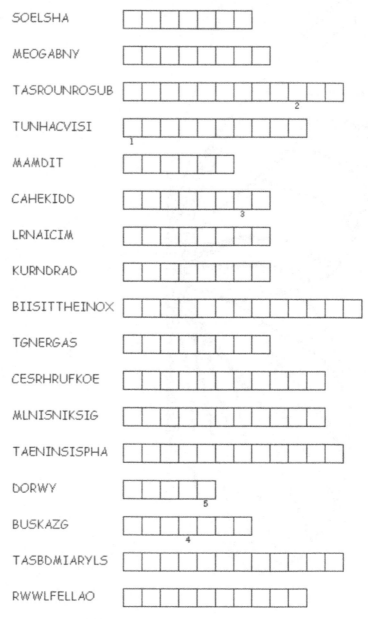

SOELSHA

MEOGABNY

TASROUNROSUB

TUNHACVISI

MAMDIT

CAHEKIDD

LRNAICIM

KURNDRAD

BIISITTHEINOX

TGNERGAS

CESRHRUFKOE

MLNISNIKSIG

TAENINSISPHA

DORWY

BUSKAZG

TASBDMIARYLS

RWWLFELLAO

Answer on page 108

This pictures fucking jacked! Draw each image to it's corresponding square to fix that goddman shit. Answer on page 108

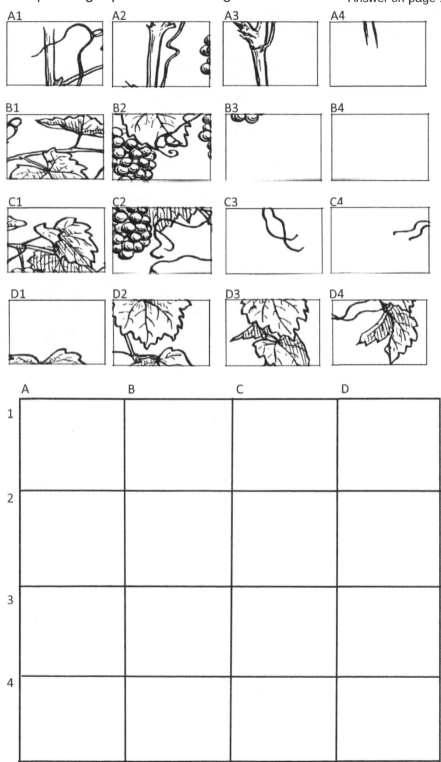

The damn goal consists of finding the black boxes in each grid.

The numbers given on the side and top of the grid indicate the numbers of consecutive black boxes in each line or column. Got that, bitches?

Here's a goddamn example: 3,3 on the left of a line indicates that there is, from left to right, a block of 3 black boxes then a block of 3 black boxes on this line. Have I lost your ass yet?
To solve a puzzle, one needs to determine which cells will be black and which will be fucking empty. Determining which cells are to be left empty (called spaces) is as important as determining which to fill (called boxes). Later in the solving process, the spaces help determine where a clue (continuing block of boxes and a number in the legend) may spread. Solvers usually use a dot or a cross to mark cells they are certain are spaces.

It is also important never to fucking guess. Only cells that can be determined by damn logic should be filled. An example is shown here:

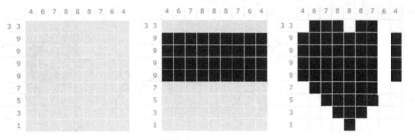

Answer on page 108

		8	1 1	1	0	8	1	8	0	8	1 1	1 1	0	8	2	2 2	1 1
3 1 1 3 1 1																	
1 1 1 1 1 1																		
2 1 1 1 1 1																		
1 1 1 1 2																		
1 1 1 1 2																		
1 1 1 1 1 1																		
1 1 1 1 1 1																		
1 3 3 1 1																		

Hey wanker! Draw lines from 100 to 180
Don't let the extra numbers fuck with your head!

Answer on
page 109

One fucking asshole always has to stand out in a crowd. Find the cunt that's different from the rest.

Answer on page 109

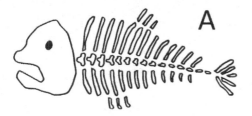

A

B

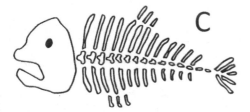

C

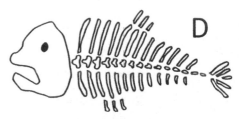

D

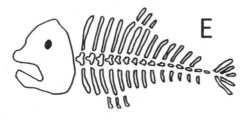

E

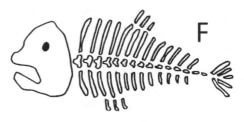

F

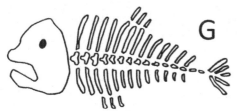

G

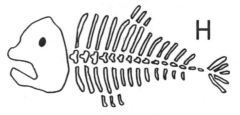

H

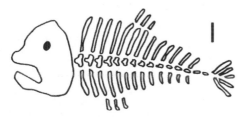

I

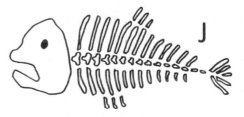

J

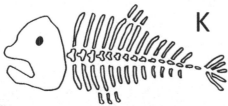

K

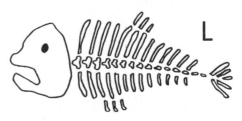

L

Ever play Sudoku? I bet your sorry ass hasn't!
These are the goddamn rules. Answer on page 109

Numbers from 1 to 9 are inserted into sets that have 9 x 9 = 81 squares in whole. Every number can be used just once in every, 3x3 block, column and row, so don't reuse that shit.

- Every number can be used just once in the blocks of 3 x 3 = 9 square blocks. Use a number more than once, you fuck everything up.
- Each row of 9 numbers ought to contain all digits 1 through 9 in any order, so don't fucking miss any.
- Every column of 9 numbers should comprise all digits 1 through 9 in any order. Hope you can fucking count.

Here's a hint for your stupid ass: One way to figure out which numbers can go in each space is to use "process of elimination" by checking to see which other numbers are already included within each square – remember, no duplicates, asshole.

		2		9		4		5
		4		8				
3		9	2	4	5			
			1					7
	6	5		2		9	3	
7					9			
			3	5	4	6		8
				7		1		
4		8		1		5		

Bet your ass you can't find the image
hidden in the picture below.
Think you can? Color that shit in!
Then see if you're right.

Answer on page 109

These pictures are not the same, douchebag!
Circle the 14 differences.

Answer on page 109

Here are the damn rules of a cryptogram:

You are given a fucked piece of text where each letter is substituted with a irrelevant damn number and you need to fucking decide which letter in the native alphabet is being coded by the numbers you are given.

You need to use logic and knowledge of the letters and words of our goddamn language to crack this shit or your fucked.

Here's a hint for your dumbass. One of the words is: *Much*

Answer on page 109

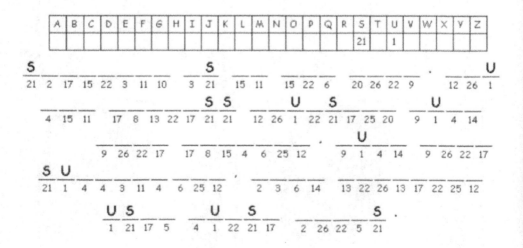

Number Blocks

Answer on page 109

Try to fill in the missing numbers if you can, asshole!

The missing numbers are integers (that means it's a whole number, dumbass) between 0 and 18.
The numbers in each row add up to the totals to the right.
The numbers in each column add up to the totals along the bottom. Numbers can be repeated, so don't get fucked and don't be an ass!
The diagonal lines also add up the totals to the right.
Good fucking luck!

						59
13					14	55
19	2	13		8		45
	10		8	18	20	69
7			2		2	30
0		14	18	10		61
	10		11	2	20	73
60	46	60	52	46	69	51

Find the one fucking image that is different from the rest.

Answer on page 109

A	B	C	D

E	F	G	H

I	J	K	L

M	N	O	P

Q	R	S	T

U	V	W	X

Answer on page 110

Solve this bitch of a maze. Start in the opening on the top and work your way to the center. Don't fucking cheat your way out.

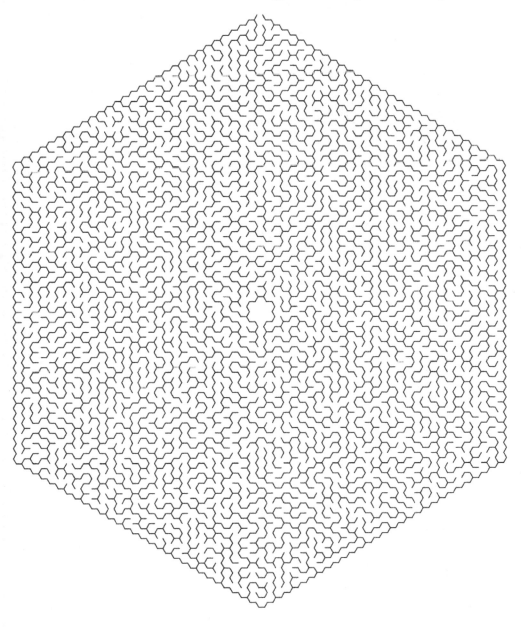

Draw the other half, jackass, and don't fuck it up.

Ever play Sudoku? I bet your ridiculous ass hasn't!
Here are the mother fucking rules.

Answer on page 110

Numbers from 1 to 9 are inserted into sets that have 9 x 9 = 81 squares in whole. Every number can be used just once in every, 3x3 block, column and row, so don't reuse that shit.

- Every number can be used just once in the blocks of 3 x 3 = 9 square blocks. Use a number more than once, you fuck shit up.
- Each row of 9 numbers ought to contain all digits 1 through 9 in any order, so don't leave out any numbers, asshole.
- Every column of 9 numbers should comprise all digits 1 through 9 in any order. Hope you got all that that shit.

Here's a hint jackass: One way to figure out which numbers can go in each space is to use "process of elimination" by checking to see which other numbers are already included within each square – remember, no duplicates, dumbass.

6			8					
		1		6	3			
3		4	5				1	6
	1		3	4			5	
		6		8		3		
	3			5	2		9	
8	9				5	7		1
			9	3		8		
					8			9

Search for the jacked up words

Answer on page 110

Butt
Coky
Prick
Skunk
Thief
Wino

Cretin
Brainy
Nobody
Fanny
Rufian
Macho

Asswipe
Fuckhead
Helldog
Donkey
Oddball

```
Q S A N E Y M N Q J M I M M Q W F V F R
O X D J X W Z D G I A P C P C I W K H U
Y J D L J H W G E I G A A C I N D O H F
I B J H L A B J J M H E S V O O I J J I
T N Y A C W M D D S C N Z E K K O R L A
C R H G U Z F B R W W Z Z A K T Y F X N
N H B E W Y S P R A I W M N V Z K H V D
S T T K H E L L D O G X K D N E I D R J
S D H F S H E A A L K Y S H F D A O D T
I A L D F P O H H O J X D H A K Y O E G
E N E K U B U T T R I R H O R I N Y T F
G O A E X Q T M L N R O C A B K L T D C
T X S E O T V F G H V P R V E O E F A T
U U A B O K P I Z E O B D Y J I N J U P
F I S X O F T A W X I C X G P Y L F N V
O U X D Y P U V A W Y E D Q U L B Y B P
F L C L V I R M S M Q O Z Q C L S N R W
S J S K U N K F S M W Y F E X I E I Y N
U R I Y H Z S P W I L S N T G E C A X G
T W N T S E Z X I Z D S B N Q K K R Q N
Y G O O H C A M P O U B X D Z Q O B F J
Y Z C C N P U D E H A O T A Z V C L F N
M A U N G S C R E T I N D T B L Q W A Q
G H G J S V F B K T U F I D U L A E E U
V O W L K B S Z I K J J E Z B C E F P E
U G O G M K Z D P W H M R I S A D N T O
F Q I P X M C W F R G Y N N A F L X R H
N X G J Q D Y S V R E L D H A E F L A W
P J R T O D L U T N R Y H S Q F E I H T
F Z W Y U V D B A D G N D S W U X E O W
```

Tell me how many stars you see in the image, bitch!

Answer on page 110

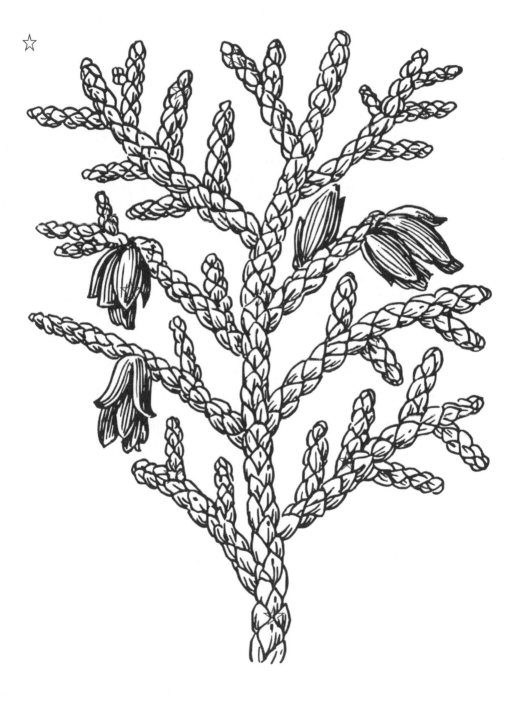

Draw some goddamn lines from 100 to 173
Don't get fucked by the extra numbers!

Answer on page 110

230
218
278   240
276   260
258   268
121 243
233 233 248 264
120
244   272
245
246   242
118 119 122 123
238   246   223
249
117   124
254   247
243 245   250   237   237
253
251   257   255   272   239   125
254   279   255   274
130 129 128 126
265   236   127
270   226   254   275
271
248   185   238
230   249
262   264   131   237
238   258   116 236
256   250   259   257   265   200
241   272
242   269   239   212   243
259   239   241   247   269   266
214   115   210
244   267
239   253   262 114   132 241
222   113 195   239   260   269
237   271   268
237   236 259   226 112 261   250   245   270
236   268 225   111   196   256   133   263
110 211   239   277
235   197   134 174
212   275   263
217 109   210   198   188 175   240
235   266   207 209   238
236 248 176   177
279   278   261
270   215   213   271   189 199   135   187 178
108   186   181   179
238   214   217   273 136
234   265   276   273   184 183 182
228   264   206 148 137   180
260   107   169   160   159   149   275   194   213
263   277 278   256   215 138
106   216   231   218   273 267 237 249   224
105   220   261   209   201   193
104 170 168   227   247 150   266   274   246 252
262   171   208 139   274 252
167 161   158 151 229   140
228   276   238   152   147 141 202 192
234   224 252   244   225 146   251
190   279   166   227   191
103   257   216   157   255   205   211
172 267   165 162   258   236   231
102   204   156   142   220
101   153   273 143 229
100 173   251   164 163 155 154   253   145 144   222
240   203

76

One fucking asshole always has to be different. Find that dick.

Answer on page 110

This picture's fucked! Draw each image to its corresponding square to fix this shit or we are all fucked.

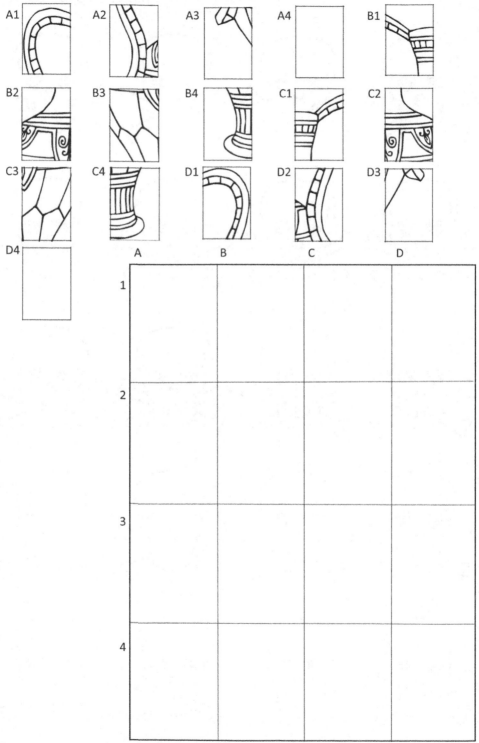

Answer on page 111

Fallen Phrases

Answer on page 111

A fallen phrase is a fucked puzzle where all the letters have fallen to the bottom. They got jacked up on their way down, but remain in the same row. Complete this jacked up shit by filling the letters in the column they fall under. You start by filling in the one-letter columns, because those clearly don't have anywhere else to go in their column, asswipe. Don't make this shit harder than it has to be.

Also try filling in common one-, two- and three-letter words. I even gave your lucky ass an example.

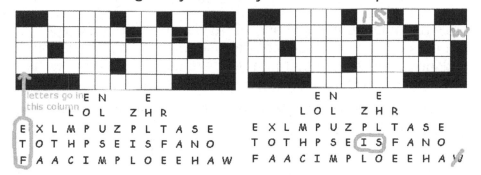

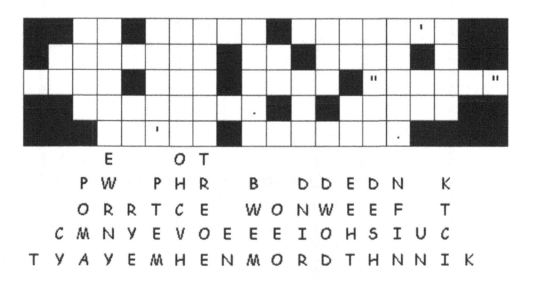

Ever play Sudoku? I bet your sorry ass hasn't! These are the goddamn rules.

Answer on page 111

Numbers from 1 to 9 are inserted into sets that have 9 x 9 = 81 squares in whole. Every number can be used just once in every, 3x3 block, column and row, so don't reuse that shit.

- Every number can be used just once in the blocks of 3 x 3 = 9 square blocks. Use a number more than once, you fuck everything up.
- Each row of 9 numbers ought to contain all digits 1 through 9 in any order, so don't fucking miss any.
- Every column of 9 numbers should comprise all digits 1 through 9 in any order. Hope you can fucking count.

Here's a hint for your stupid ass: One way to figure out which numbers can go in each space is to use "process of elimination" by checking to see which other numbers are already included within each square – remember, no duplicates, asshole.

3		7	1		2			8
				9		7		6
	5					1		
2	8		1				7	
	3					6		
	4		8			5	9	
		8				3		
4		3	5					
1			4		7	9		2

The fucked rules of a cryptogram puzzle:

You are given a shit piece of text where each letter is substituted with a irrelevant damn number and you need to fucking decide which letter in the native alphabet is being coded by the numbers you are given.

You need to use logic and knowledge of the letters and words of our goddamn language to crack this shit.

Here's a fucking hint.
One of the words is:
trouble

Answer on page 111

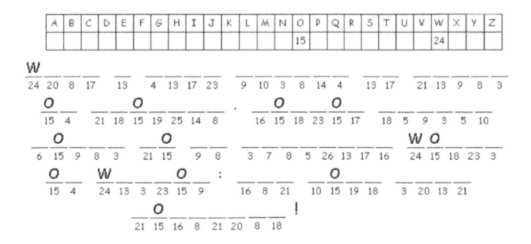

A	B	C	D	E	F	G	H	I	J	K	L	M	N	O	P	Q	R	S	T	U	V	W	X	Y	Z
														15								24			

W
24 20 8 17   13   4 13 17 23   9 10 3   8 14 4   13 17   21 13 9 8 3

O   O   ,   O   O
15 4   21 18 15 19 25 14 8   16 15 18 23 15 17   18 5 9 3 5 10

   O   O   W O
6 15 9 8 3   21 15   9 8   3 7 8 5 26 13 17 16   24 15 18 23 3

   O   W   O   :   O
15 4   24 13 3 23 15 9   16 8 21   10 15 19 18   3 20 13 21

         O
21 15 16 8 21 20 8 18   !

I can't read these fucking words. Unscramble the fuck out of them. Take the letters that appear in numbered boxes to reveal the fucking last word.

Answer on page 111

IYOFRANPT

SI

HET

NAETELBIIV

LIUNICSGTI

TUHRCC

FO

CINTIETARLUA.

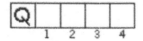

Circle the 10 fucking differences. Can you find them all, bitch?

Answer on page 111

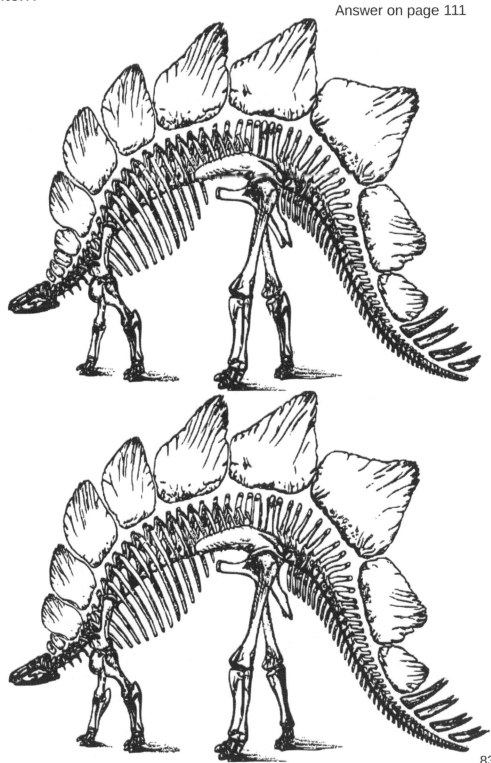

Answer on page 111

Solve the maze. Start in the opening on the left and work your way to the goddamn opening in the center of the triangle. Get lost? Check the fucking back, dumbass!

The goal of this puzzle is to figure out how the hell you fit the numbered rectangles into the motherfucking large rectangle. And don't even think about splitting those fuckers apart, you goddamn cheater!

Answer on page 112

| 4 | 4 | 4 |
| 4 | 4 | 4 |

8	8
8	8
8	8

| 2 |
| 2 |
| 2 |
| 2 |

| 7 | 7 | 7 |
| | 7 | |

| 10 | 10 |
| 10 | 10 | 10 | 10 |

| 5 |
| 5 | 5 |
| 5 | 5 |

| 3 |
| 3 | 3 |

| 6 | 6 |
| 6 | 6 |

| 9 |
| 9 |
| 9 | 9 | 9 |

| 1 |
| 1 |
| 1 | 1 |
| 1 | 1 |

Letter Tiles

I can't fucking read this shit!

Move the goddamn tiles around to
make the correct phrase.

The three letters on each tile must
stay together and in the given order,
so don't try to cheat, asswipe!

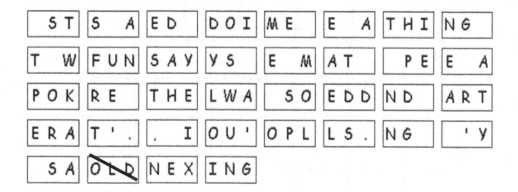

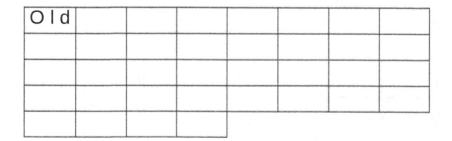

Have fucking fun coloring, bitch!

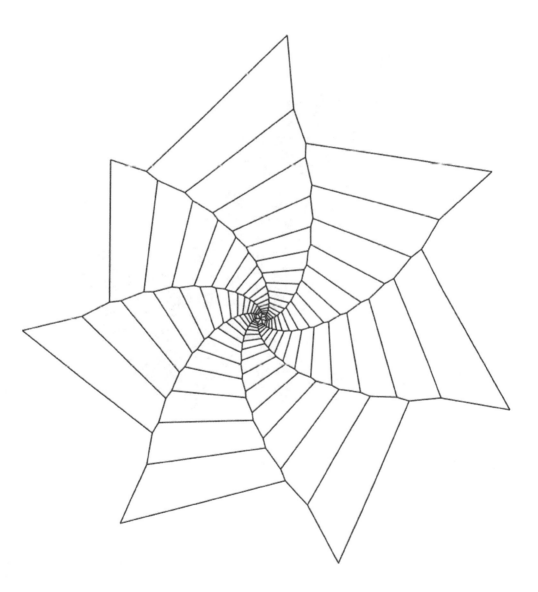

How many goddamn dots can you find?
(This one fucks with the eyes)

Answer on page 112

Find the fucker that's different from the rest.

Answer on page 112

This picture's fucked to hell! Draw each image to its corresponding square to fix that shit.

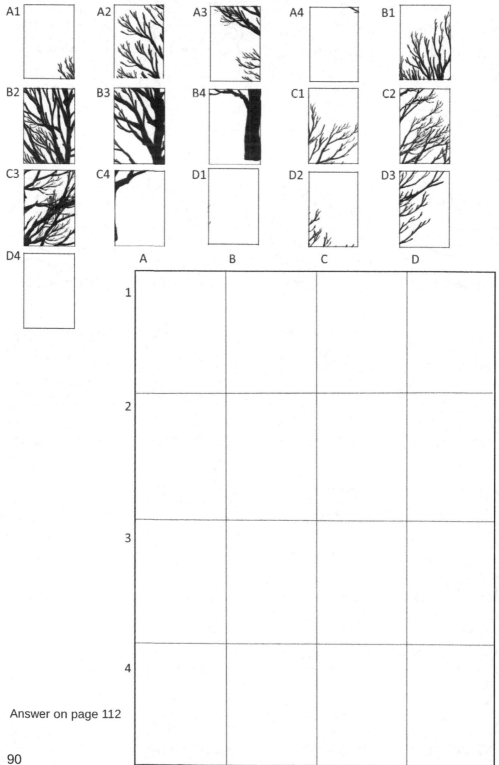

Answer on page 112

Spot the 12 differences between the images, crazy bitches!

Answer on page 112

Connect the fucking numbers from 100 to 127
Extra numbers? You bet your sweet ass there are!

Answer on page 112

161
218
129
230 114 115
116 240 278 276
128
151
162
258
268 113
248 264
243
245
244
223 233
246
242
131
238 246
249
238
254
243 245 247
250
237 150
237
154
257
233
253
149
251
254
255
279 255
274 272
239
265
270
226
254
275
236
135
271
159 248
185
166
249
165 230
168 167
262
264
137
238 160
258 132 236
265
256
250
259
257 169
272
138
242 269
241 239
212
243
259 239
241
214
247
210
269 266
244
171
267
253 110 111 112 262
117 118 170 241
239
239
153
109
222
195
119 120 260 136
237
237
268
236 259
226
261 172 250 245
236
196 256
121 263
268 225
211 239
277
271
174
235 217
197
236
263
155
156 275
240
107 108
212
210
198 188 175
235
266 130
207 209
173 238
177
106
236 248 176
279
278 261
157
215 213 271
189 199
187 178
133
214
186 181 179
105
146
260
180
234 238
276 273
184 183 182
228 163
217
200
213
260 104
264 206
269 275 194
263
215
122
278 256
218 273 267 237
139
277 103
216 231 209
201
193
270 220 261
266 274 246 123
227 247
262 279
237 270 229
208
224
124 252
158 140
238
228
202 192 249
234
102
225 190
251
224 252 244
242
274 191
142
227
211
272 144
147 255 205 231
257
216
145
267
101
258
252
220
143
204 148 152
273
229
134 251
100
253
125 222
127 276
141
240 126 203 164

92

Answer on page 113

Search for the goddamn motherfucking words

Ape	Balls	Creep	Bozo
Fake	Idiot	Dufus	Tit
Liar	Minx	Joker	Snot
Nurd	Pig	Satan	Sack

```
U W E I J M                              S Z Y O Q L
P J O K E R                              I Z O Q N R
 J F J B A S                            M H R O R M
 G J G W O S                            C J M V J F
  G B V C Z Q                          L G N Y I W
  Q N A P E O                          W W P V V H
   D A O T I Q                        O T E E D H
   T V T F O M                        I V J E W T
    F B A P I R                      T H P K R O
    R L C S W D                      Q F K O C M
     F R K M E I                    R L K D W E
     P B C I O I                    D B R Q W R
      S A N T B J                  N U R D N A
      H S X I Z Z                  T I B N I Z
       V P B S L N          D C J J L S
       I I Z S V X          J D U T G Q
        M B U A Y Q      X O S C I N
        Q X X B V Y      E K J Z T R
         Q K O U J L H W E K A F
         U P S L L A B I P U F M
          X O H P P R C I X G
          W K I D S H U G K J
           Y R U N O F M S
           K T F O B I X B
            G U T D E P
            X S A G F P
             E Z W Z
             P T S S
```

How many fucking hearts can you find?

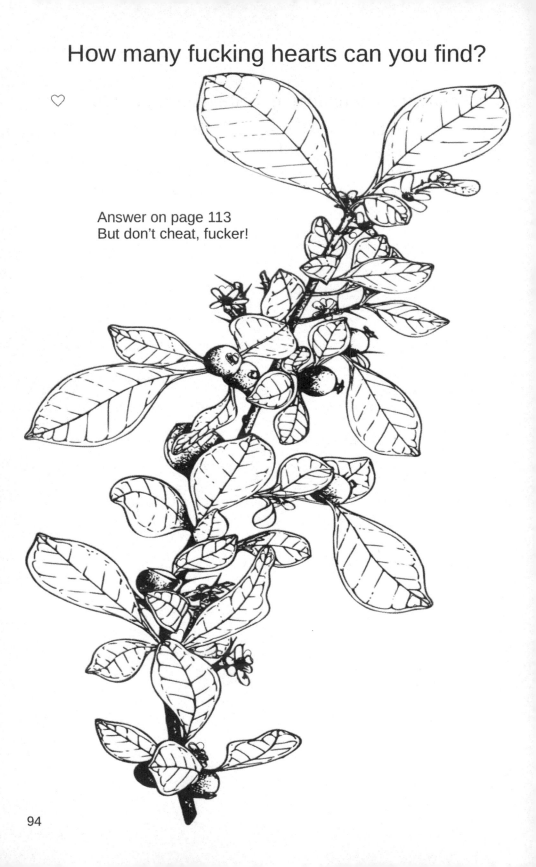

Answer on page 113
But don't cheat, fucker!

Color this shit!

Word Scramble

Answer on page 113

I can't read these wacked words. Unscramble the fuckers. Take the letters that appear in numbered boxes to reveal the best damn word.

LOYH JUSSE NO A KITCS

TOCCISHK CEERHTOURFKM

A RITMEC FUKC-ONT

NFGIKCU HUNCB FO ISTIOD

TAHDISLO

FUKC ME TCIWE NO NAYSUDS

MOHRET-HIST-KUCF

GO SISP PU A EOPR

KUFC YUO

HYOL KFNUNCAFREK

WERHE IN TIACOUKPF

KLFACBULS

Here are the damn rules of a cryptogram:

You are given a fucked piece of text where each letter is substituted with a irrelevant damn number and you need to fucking decide which letter in the native alphabet is being coded by the numbers you are given.

You need to use logic and knowledge of the letters and words of our goddamn language to crack this shit or your fucked.

Answer on page 113

Here's a hint fucker:
One of the words *Insecure*

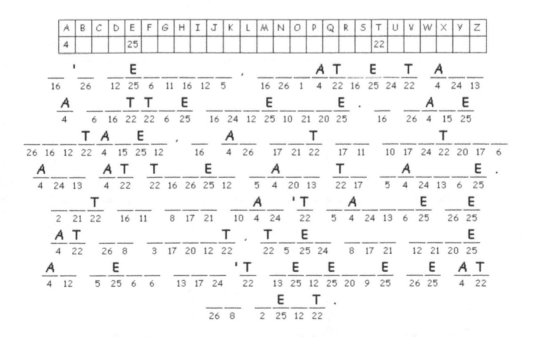

Ever play Sudoku? I bet you fucking haven't! Answer on page 113
These are the wanked rules.

Numbers from 1 to 9 are inserted into sets that have 9 x 9 = 81 squares in whole. Every number can be used just once in every, 3x3 block, column and row, so don't reuse the goddamn shit.

- Every number can be used just once in the blocks of 3 x 3 = 9 square blocks. Use a number more than once, your fucked.
- Each row of 9 numbers must fucking contain all digits 1 through 9 in any order, so don't fucking miss that shit.
- Every column of 9 numbers should comprise all digits 1 through 9 in any order. Hope you can fucking count, bitch.

Here's a hint for your stupid ass: One way to figure out which numbers can go in each space is to use "process of elimination" by checking to see which other numbers are already included within each square – remember, no duplicates, asshole.

		1		7	8			6
	9						1	
6				1	3		4	
9		8	7					5
			5		9			
1					4	3		7
	6		1	5				3
	1						8	
7			4	8		2		

Start at the top and work your way the fuck down to
the bottom, jackass!

Answer on page 113

Fallen Phrases

Answer on page 113

A fallen phrase is a fucked puzzle where all the letters have fallen to the bottom. They got jacked up on their way down, but remain in the same row. Complete this fucked up shit by filling the letters in the column they fall under. You start by filling in the one-letter columns, because those clearly don't have anywhere else to go in their column, dumbass. Don't make this shit harder than it has to be.
Also try filling in common one-, two- and three-letter words. I even gave your lucky ass an example.

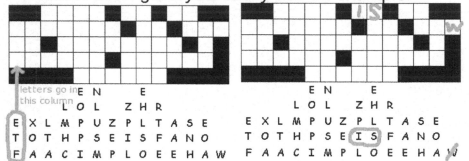

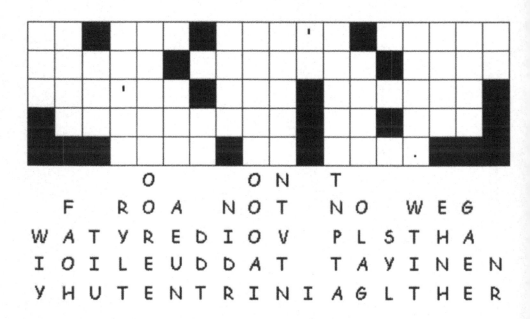

Page 1

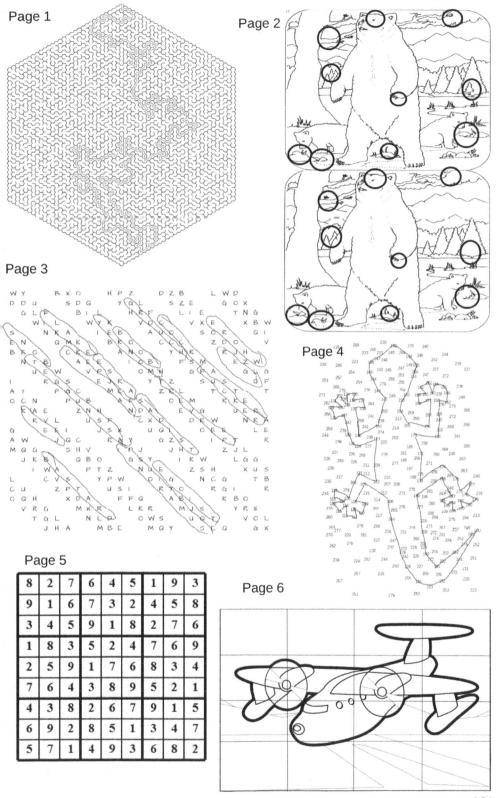

Page 2

Page 3

Page 4

Page 5

8	2	7	6	4	5	1	9	3
9	1	6	7	3	2	4	5	8
3	4	5	9	1	8	2	7	6
1	8	3	5	2	4	7	6	9
2	5	9	1	7	6	8	3	4
7	6	4	3	8	9	5	2	1
4	3	8	2	6	7	9	1	5
6	9	2	8	5	1	3	4	7
5	7	1	4	9	3	6	8	2

Page 6

Page 8

Page 9

315 total fists

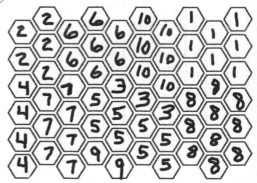

Page 11

People who use a lot of swear words tend to be more honest and trustworthy, human behavioral studies suggest.

Page 10

Page 12

Page 13

When I say 'I understand' it doesn't mean I understand, It doesn't mean I agree, it doesn't even mean I'm Listening. -Two and a Half Men

Page 14

2	8	7	6	4	5	9	3	1
5	4	9	1	3	8	7	6	2
1	6	3	9	2	7	8	5	4
3	1	2	4	8	9	6	7	5
4	9	5	7	6	2	3	1	8
8	7	6	3	5	1	2	4	9
9	5	4	8	7	6	1	2	3
6	2	8	5	1	3	4	9	7
7	3	1	2	9	4	5	8	6

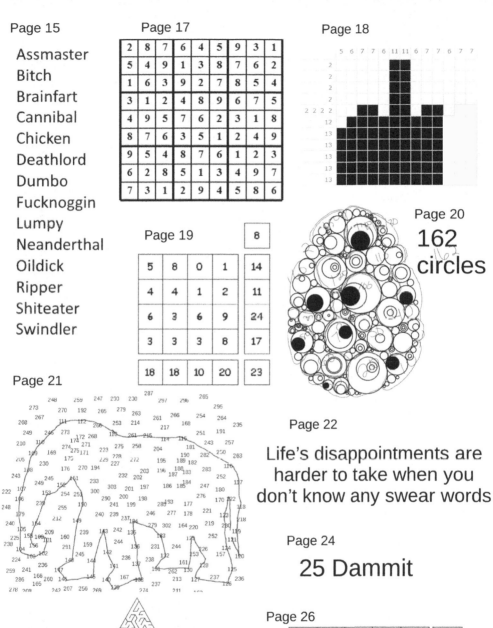

				8
5	8	0	1	14
4	4	1	2	11
6	3	6	9	24
3	3	3	8	17
18	18	10	20	23

162 circles

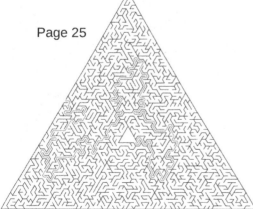

Life's disappointments are harder to take when you don't know any swear words

25 Dammit

2	+	8	×	1	10
+		/		×	
9	+	4	-	7	6
+		+		-	
6	×	5	+	3	33
17		7		4	

Page 28

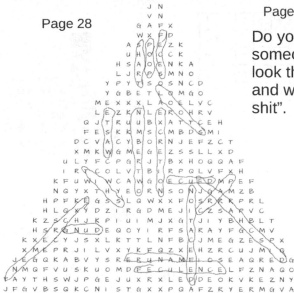

Page 29

Do you ever just wanna grab someone by the shoulders, look them deep in the eyes and whisper "No one gives a shit".

Page 30

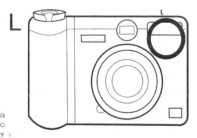

Page 31

You call them "Cuss words" I choose to call them "Sentence enhancers".

Page 32

5	9	8	7	2	1	4	3	6
6	7	1	3	4	5	8	2	9
4	2	3	6	8	9	7	5	1
2	3	7	8	9	4	1	6	5
9	8	4	5	1	6	2	7	3
1	6	5	2	7	3	9	8	4
8	4	6	9	3	2	5	1	7
7	5	9	1	6	8	3	4	2
3	1	2	4	5	7	6	9	8

Page 33

Page 34

483 Butterfly

They're= They Fucking Are
Their = Shows Fucking Possession
There = Specifies a Fucking Location
You're = You Fucking Is
Your = Shows Fucking Possession
We're = We Fucking Are
Were = Past Fucking Tense of Are
Where = Specifies a Fucking Location
Loose = Not Fucking Fixed In Place
Lose = Cease To Fucking Keep
Affect = A Fucking Action
Effect = A Fucking Result
Could've = Could Fucking Have
Could of = You're A Fucking Idiot

The Best

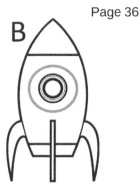

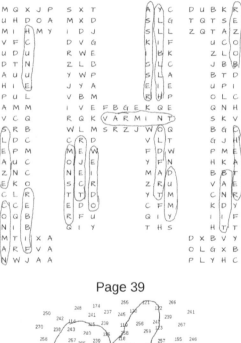

105

Page 41

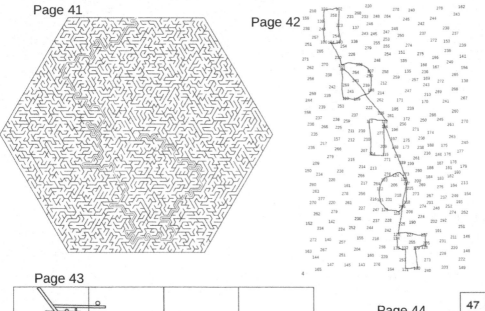

Page 42

Page 43

Page 44

14	12	9	8	10	53
3	4	12	10	5	34
1	2	8	12	10	33
4	10	1	3	1	19
9	13	1	1	0	24
31	41	31	34	26	29

47

Page 45

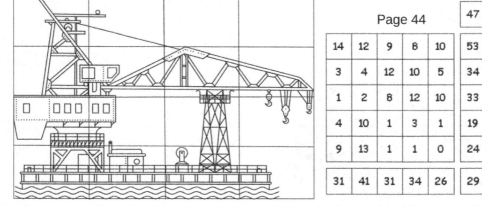

I can tell by your sarcastic
Undertones, rude comments
and sheer lack of common
decency that we should be
best friends.

Page 49

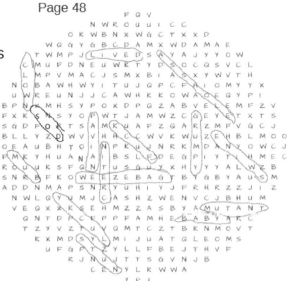

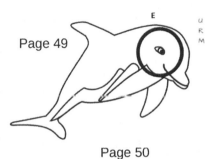

Page 50

Swearing. Because sometimes
"gosh darn" and "poopy head"
just don't cover it!

Page 52

Page 51

1	-	7	-	2	-	6	-14
-		+		X		X	
15	+	10	+	4	X	12	73
X		-		-		/	
8	-	11	X	9	/	3	-25
+		+		-		-	
16	-	13	-	5	-	14	-16
135		19		-6		10	

Page 53

5	8	1	9	7	4	2	3	6
9	2	4	6	5	3	1	7	8
7	3	6	1	2	8	5	4	9
6	7	2	5	3	1	8	9	4
4	5	8	2	9	6	7	1	3
1	9	3	8	4	7	6	2	5
2	6	5	3	1	9	4	8	7
3	1	7	4	8	5	9	6	2
8	4	9	7	6	2	3	5	1

Page 54
If anybody even tries to whisper
The word 'Diet' I'm like.
"You can go fuck yourself".

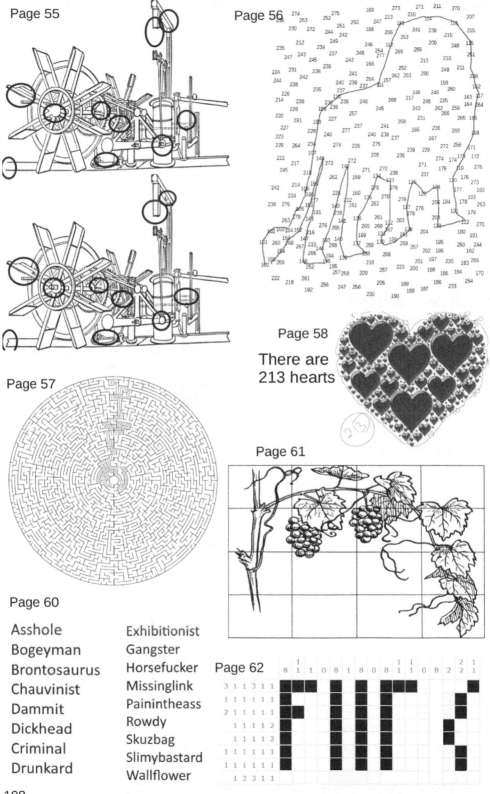

Page 55

Page 56

Page 58

There are
213 hearts

Page 57

Page 61

Page 60

Asshole
Bogeyman
Brontosaurus
Chauvinist
Dammit
Dickhead
Criminal
Drunkard

Exhibitionist
Gangster
Horsefucker
Missinglink
Painintheass
Rowdy
Skuzbag
Slimybastard
Wallflower

Page 62

1	7	2	6	9	3	4	8	5
6	5	4	7	8	1	3	2	9
3	8	9	2	4	5	7	1	6
9	4	3	1	6	8	2	5	7
8	6	5	4	2	7	9	3	1
7	2	1	5	3	9	8	6	4
2	1	7	3	5	4	6	9	8
5	9	6	8	7	2	1	4	3
4	3	8	9	1	6	5	7	2

Swearing is an art form. You can express yourself much more exactly, much more succinctly, with properly used curse words

13	7	2	12	7	14	59
19	2	13	1	8	2	55
9	10	4	8	18	20	45
7	9	9	2	1	2	69
0	8	14	18	10	11	30
12	10	18	11	2	20	61
60	46	60	52	46	69	73
						51

6	2	9	8	1	4	5	7	3
5	7	1	2	6	3	9	8	4
3	8	4	5	9	7	2	1	6
7	1	2	3	4	9	6	5	8
9	5	6	7	8	1	3	4	2
4	3	8	6	5	2	1	9	7
8	9	3	4	2	5	7	6	1
1	4	7	9	3	6	8	2	5
2	6	5	1	7	8	4	3	9

```
Q S A N E Y M N Q J M I  M M Q W F V F
O X D J X W Z D G I  A P C P C I W K H
Y J D L J H W G E I  G A A C I N D O H
I  B J H L A B J J M H E S V O I  J J I
T N Y A C W M D D S C N Z E K K O R L
C R H G U Z F B R W W Z Z A K T Y F X N
N H B E W Y S P R A I  W M N V Z K H V D
S T T K H E L L D O G X K D N E I  D R J
S D H F S H E A A L K Y S H F D A O D T
I  A L D F P O H H O J X D H A K Y O E G
E N E K U B U T T R I  R H O R I  N Y T F
G O A E X Q T M L N R O C A B K L T D C
T X S E O T V F G H V P R V E O E F A T
U U A B O K P I  Z E O B D Y J N J U P
I  S X O F T A W X I  C X G P Y L F N V
O U X D Y P U V A W Y E D Q U L B Y B P
F L C L V I  R M S M Q O Z Q C L S N R W
S J S K U N K F S M W Y F E X I  E I  Y N
U R I  Y H Z S P W I  L S N T G E C A X G
T W N T S E Z X I  Z D S B N Q K K R Q N
Y G O O H C A M P O U B X D Z Q O B F J
Y Z C C N P U D E H A O T A Z V C L F N
M A U N G S C R E T I  N D T B L Q W A Q
G H G J S V F B K T U F I  D U L A E E U
V O W L K B S Z I  K J J E Z B R E F P E
U G O G M K Z D P W H M R I  S A D N T O
F Q I  P X M C W F R G Y N N A F I  X R H
N X G J Q D Y S V R E L D H A E F L A W
P J R T O D L U T N R Y H S Q F E I  H T
F Z W Y U V D B A D G N D S W U X E O W
```

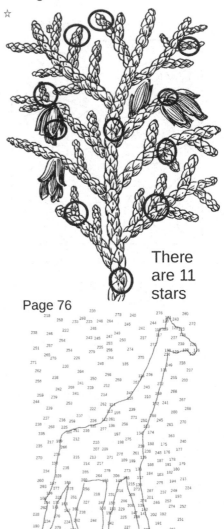

There are 11 stars

G

110

Page 78

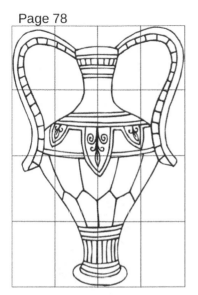

Page 79

My phone doesn't correct me when
I type the word "fuck" anymore.
I think we've bonded.

Page
80

3	9	7	1	6	2	5	4	8
8	1	4	5	9	3	7	2	6
6	5	2	7	4	8	1	9	3
2	8	6	9	1	5	3	7	4
5	3	9	2	7	4	8	6	1
7	4	1	3	8	6	2	5	9
9	7	8	6	2	1	4	3	5
4	2	3	8	5	9	6	1	7
1	6	5	4	3	7	9	8	2

Page 81

When I find myself in times
of trouble Gordon Ramsay
comes to me speaking
words of wisdom: Get Your
Shit Together

Page 82

Profanity
is
The
Inevitable
Linguistic
Crutch
of
Inarticulate.

Page 83

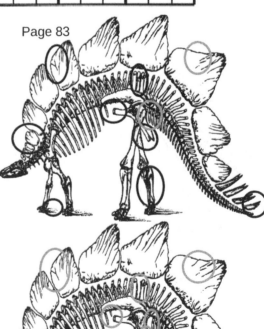

Page 84

1	4	4	4	7	7	7
1	4	4	4	3	7	2
1	1	10	10	3	3	2
1	1	10	10	10	10	2
9	6	6	8	8	5	2
9	6	6	8	8	5	5
9	9	9	8	8	5	5

Page 86

Old people at weddings always poke me and say "you're next". So, I started doing the same thing at funerals.

Page 88

Page 89

R

Page 90

12

Page 91

Page 92

112

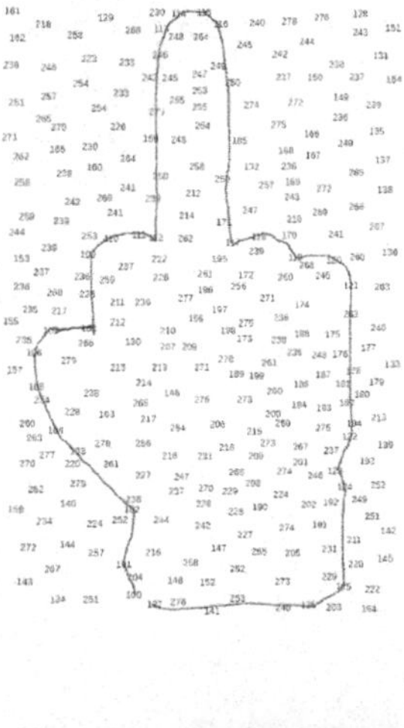

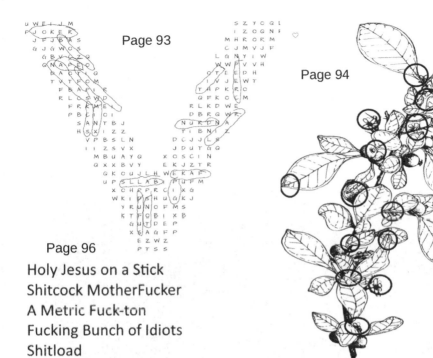

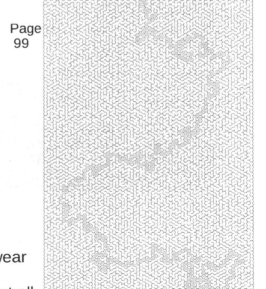

Page 94

Page 96

Holy Jesus on a Stick

Shitcock MotherFucker

A Metric Fuck-ton

Fucking Bunch of Idiots

Shitload

Fuck Me Twice on Sundays

Mother-Shit-Fuck

Go Piss Up a Rope

Fuck You

Holy Frankenfuck

Where in Fucktopia

Fuckballs

Fuck

Page 97

I'm selfish, impatient and a little insecure. I make mistakes, I am out of control and at times hard to handle. But if you can't handle me at my worst, then you sure as hell don't deserve me at my best.

Page 98

2	4	1	9	7	8	5	3	6
3	9	7	6	4	5	8	1	2
6	8	5	2	1	3	7	4	9
9	2	8	7	3	1	4	6	5
4	7	3	5	6	9	1	2	8
1	5	6	8	2	4	3	9	7
8	6	4	1	5	2	9	7	3
5	1	2	3	9	7	6	8	4
7	3	9	4	8	6	2	5	1

Page 99

Page 100   If you don't swear while driving then you're not paying attention to the road at all.

So you finished that whole fuckload of activities? Bet you feel fucking accomplished. Bet you feel like a goddamn genius. Well wipe that smirk off your cunt mouth. Here's another book of shit to do in case you're STILL FUCKING BORED! Now you don't have to waste away the hours pleasuring yourself, wishing there was a fucking better way to keep your mind and hands busy. I've even added some new types of activities, since you're a motherfucking expert now.

Let's face it, you can't get enough of this shit. So here, take my crowbar, pry open your fucking wallet, and show those assholes you aren't as goddamn cheap as they say you are.

Check out these other fun fucking items by the Author:

Books by Tamara L Adams
Angry Journal
Art Up This Journal
Art Up This Journal #2
Activititties
Activity Book for Adults
Activity Book You Never Knew You Wanted But Can't Live Without
Activity Book You need to Buy Before You Die
Fuck I'm Bored : Adult Activity Book
The Activity Book That Will Transform Your Life
Activities to do while you number two
Timmy and the Dragon
Pebble pal pete
Unmotivated Coloring
Angry Coloring
Coloring Happy Quotes
Inspirational Quotes Coloring
Coloring Cocktails
Cussing Creatures Color
101 Quote Inspired Journal Prompts
76 Quote Inspired Journal Prompts
51 Quote Inspired Journal Prompts
Unlocking Happiness Planner
Daily Fitness Planner
Bloggers Daily Planner
Bloggers Daily Planner w margins
Writers Daily Planner
Writers Daily Planner w coloring
Busy Mothers Planner
Where's Woody Coloring Book
M.A.S.H.
99 Writing Prompts
Deciding Destiny: Christy's Choice
Deciding Destiny: Matt's Choice
Deciding Destiny: Lindsays Choice
Deciding Destiny: Joe's Choice
Rich Stryker: Julie's Last Hope
Rich Stryker: Tom's Final Justice
Unlocking Happiness
Getting to Know Yourself Journal
#2 Getting to Know Yourself Journal

Thanks for your goddman purchase!!

Please leave a review! I would be fucking grateful.

Contact me to get a free printable PDF of Activities here at:

http://www.tamaraladamsauthor.com/free-printable-activity-book-pdf/

Tamaraadamsauthor@gmail.com

Thank you for your support and have a great fucking day!

You can contact me at

http://www.amazon.com/T.L.-Adams/e/B00YSROGC4

Tammy@tamaraladamsauthor.com

https://www.pinterest.com/TamaraLAdamsAuthor/

https://twitter.com/TamaraLAdams

https://www.facebook.com/TamaraLAdamsAuthor/

https://www.youtube.com/user/tamaraladams

https://www.instagram.com/tamaraladamsauthor/

http://www.tamaraladamsauthor.com

Made in the USA
Monee, IL
11 March 2021

62516205R00066